Internet of Things

Rolf H. Weber • Romana Weber

Internet of Things

Legal Perspectives

Springer

Professor Dr. Rolf H. Weber
Professor for Civil, Business
and European Law
Faculty of Law
University of Zürich
Rämistraße 74/38
CH-8001 Zürich
rolf.weber@rwi.uzh.ch

Romana Weber
Nordstraße 323
CH-8037 Zürich

ISBN 978-3-642-11709-1 e-ISBN 978-3-642-11710-7
DOI 10.1007/978-3-642-11710-7
Springer Heidelberg Dordrecht London New York

ISBN 978-3-7255-5989-3
www.schulthess.com

Library of Congress Control Number: 2010927403

Published by Springer-Verlag Berlin Heidelberg 2010

Cover design: WMXDesign GmbH

Printed on acid-free paper

Springer is part of Springer Science+Business Media (www.springer.com)

Preface

The Internet of Things as an emerging global Internet-based information architecture facilitating the exchange of goods and services is gradually developing. While the technology of the Internet of Things is still being discussed and created, the legal framework should be established before the Internet of Things is fully operable, in order to allow for an effective introduction of the new information architecture. If a self-regulatory approach is to be adopted to provide a legal framework for the Internet of Things, and this seems preferable, rulemakers can draw on experiences from the current regime of Internet governance. In the near future, mainly businesses will operate in the Internet of Things. Civil society is only expected to make use of the Internet of Things, as it now does of the Internet, at a later stage (e.g. for healthcare).

The Internet of Things will have an impact in various areas. The regulatory framework must provide for provisions ensuring the security of the structure as well as the privacy of its users. Furthermore, legal barriers that may stand in the way of the coming into operation of the Internet of Things will have to be considered. However, the Internet of Things will also have positive effects in different fields, such as the inclusion of developing countries in global trade, the use of search engines to the benefit of civil society, combating product counterfeiting, tackling environmental concerns, improving health conditions, securing food supply and monitoring compliance with labor standards.

This book has benefited from many inputs and encouragements from colleagues that we are deeply grateful for. In particular, we are indebted to the very meaningful discussions and valuable support in the preparation of the publication by research assistant Ulrike I. Heinrich, and to David O'Hare for the review of the manuscript. We would also like to thank Stephan Haller for his inputs in the technological part of this book. Furthermore, we are grateful to the Ecoscentia Foundation for financially supporting the research project.

Any comments and suggestions from readers would be highly appreciated (rolf.weber@rwi.uzh.ch).

Zurich, November 2009

Rolf H. Weber
Romana Weber

Contents

Bibliography

Ahle Ulrich, RFID im praktischen Einsatz, in: Hans-Jörg Bullinger (ed.), Internet der Dinge, Berlin 2007, 331–345.

Anderson Kenneth, Book Review: Squaring the Circle? Reconciling Sovereignty and Global Governance through Global Government Networks, Harvard Law Review, Vol. 118, 2005, 1255–1312.

Arioli Martina/Thalmann André, Einsatz von RFID im Rechtsverkehr, AJP 5/2006, 549–560.

Balakrishnan Hari/Kaashoek Frans/Darger David/Morris Robert/Stoica Ion, Looking Up Data in P2P Systems, Communications of the ACM, Vol. 46, 2003, 43–48.

Basho Kalinda, The Licensing of Our Personal Information: Is It a Solution to Internet Privacy?, California Law Review, Vol. 88, 2000, 1507–1545.

Bendrath Ralf/Jørgensen Rikke Frank, The World Summit on the Information Society – Privacy not Found?, Script-ed, Vol. 3, 2006, 355–369.

Benedek Wolfgang, Internet Governance and Human Rights, in: Wolfgang Benedek/ Veronika Bauer/Matthias C. Kettemann (eds), Internet Governance and the Information Society, Utrecht 2008, 31–49.

Benghozi Pierre-Jean/Bureau Sylvain/Massit-Folléa Françoise, L'Internet des Objets: Quels Enjeux pour l'Europe? – The Internet of Things: What Challenges for Europe?, Paris 2009.

Benhamou Bernard, Organizing Internet Architecture, available at: http://www.diplomatie.gouv.fr/en/IMG/pdf/Organizing_Internet_Architecture.pdf (Benhamou, Internet Architecture).

Benhamou Bernard, A European Governance Perspective on the Object Naming Service, Governance of Resources, available at: ftp://ftp.cordis.europa.eu/pub/fp7/ict/docs/ch1-lisbon-20071215_en.pdf (Benhamou, Governance Perspective).

Benz Arthur, Einleitung: Governance – Modebegriff oder nützliches sozialwissenschaftliches Konzept?, in: Arthur Benz (ed.), Governance – Regieren in komplexen Regelsystemen, Wiesbaden 2004, 11–28.

Bienkowski Pawel, Electromagnetic Fields Measurements – Methods and Accuracy Estimation, in: Andrzej Krawczyk/Roman Kubacki/Sławomir Wiak/Carlos Lemos Antunes (eds), Electromagnetic Fields, Health and Environment, Amsterdam 2008, 229–237.

Birkinshaw Patrick, Freedom of Information and Openness: Fundamental Human Rights?, Administrative Law Review, Vol. 58, 2006, 177–218.

Birnie Patricia W./Boyle Alan E./Redgwell Catherine, International Law & the Environment, 3rd edition Oxford 2009.

Birolini Alessandro, Reliability Engineering, 5th edition Berlin 2007.

Black Julia, Constitutionalizing Self-Regulation, Modern Law Review, Vol. 59, 1996, 24–55.

BORKING JOHN J., Privacy Standards for Trust, Weblaw-Jusletter, 3 October 2005.

BOTELHO M. FILOMENA/SANTOS A. CRISTINA/LOPES M. CARMO ET AL., Effects of Radiation in Cellular Cultures, in: Andrzej Krawczyk/Roman Kubacki/Sławomir Wiak/Carlos Lemos Antunes (eds), Electromagnetic Field, Health and Environment, Amsterdam 2008, 67–71.

BOWN CHAD P., On the Economic Success of GATT/WTO Dispute Settlement, The Review of Economics and Statistics, Vol. 86, 2004, 811–823.

BREWER ERIC A., When Everything is Searcheable, Communications of the ACM, Vol. 44, 2001, 53–55.

BROWNLIE IAN, Principles of Public International Law, 7th edition Oxford/New York 2008.

BURKERT HERBERT, Globalization – Strategies for Data Protection, Weblaw-Jusletter, 3 October 2005.

BYGRAVE LEE A./SCHIAVETTA SUSAN/THUNEM HILDE/LANGE ANNEBETH B./PHILLIPS EDWARD, The Naming Game: Governance of the Domain Name System, in: Lee A. Bygrave/Jon Bing (eds), Internet Governance – Infrastructure and Institutions, Oxford 2009, 147–212.

CAMPBELL ANGELA, Self-Regulation and the Media, Federal Communications Law Journal, Vol. 51, 1999, 711–772.

CHEON KANGSIK, Multilingualism and the Domain Name System, available at: http://www.wgig.org/docs/book/Kangsik_Cheon%20.pdf.

CHEUNG ANNE/ROLF H. WEBER, Internet Governance and the Responsibility of Internet Service Providers, Wisconsin International Law Journal, Vol. 26, 2008, 403–477.

DALAL REEPAL S., Chipping away the Constitution: The increasing use of RFID chips could lead to an erosion of privacy rights, Boston University Law Review, Vol. 86, 2005, 485–514.

DE VEY MESTDAGH KEES/RIJGERSBERG RUDOLF W., Rethinking Accountability in Cyberspace: A New Perspective on ICANN, International Review of Law, Computers & Technology, Vol. 21, 2007, 27–38.

DORIA AVRI/KLEINWÄCHTER WOLFGANG (eds), Internet Governance Forum (IGF): The First Two Years, a UNESCO Publication for the World Summit of the Information Society – Special issue co-produced with ITU and UNDESA, December 2008, available at: http://www.intgovforum.org/cms/index.php/component/content/article/57–2008igf/311-internet-governance-forum-the-first-two-years.

DOWNIE DAVID L./LEVY MARC A., The UN Environment Programme at a turning point: Options for change, in: Pamela S. Chasek (ed.), The Global Environment in the Twenty-first Century: Prospects for International Cooperation, Tokyo 2000, 355–377.

DRUEY JEAN NICOLAS, Information als Gegenstand des Rechts, Zurich 1995.

DWIVEDI O.P./JABBRA JOSEPH G., Introduction: Public Service Responsibility and Accountability, in: O.P. Dwivedi/Joseph G. Jabbra (eds), Public Service Accountability, West Hartford, Connecticut 1989, 1–16.

EBRAHIM ALNOOR/HERZ STEVE, Accountability in Complex Organizations: World Bank Responses to Civil Society, John F. Kennedy School of Government, Harvard University, December 2007, RWP 07–060, available at: http://www.hbs.edu/research/pdf/08–027.pdf.

EHRENBERG DANIEL S., The Labor Link: Applying the International Trading System to Enforce Violations of Forced and Child Labor, Yale Journal of International Law, Vol. 20, 1995, 361–417.

ESCHET GAL, Protecting Privacy in the web of Radio Frequency Identification, Jurimetrics, Vol. 45, 2005, 301–332.

EVDOKIMOV SERGEI/FABIAN BENJAMIN/GÜNTHER OLIVER, Multipolarity for the Object Naming Service, in: Christian Floerkemeier/Marc Langheinrich/Elgar Fleisch/Friedemann Mattern/Sanjay E. Sarma (eds), The Internet of Things, Berlin/Heidelberg 2008, 1–18.

FABIAN BENJAMIN, Secure Name Services for the Internet of Things, Thesis, Berlin 2008.

FABIAN BENJAMIN/GÜNTHER OLIVER, Security Challenges of the EPCglobal Network, Communications of the ACM, Vol. 52, July 2009, 121–125 (FABIAN/GÜNTHER, Security Challenges).

FABIAN BENJAMIN/GÜNTHER OLIVER, Distributed ONS and its Impact on Privacy, available at: http://ieeexplore.ieee.org/stamp/stamp.jsp?arnumber=04288878 (FABIAN/GÜNTHER, Distributed ONS).

FABIAN BENJAMIN/GÜNTHER OLIVER/SPIEKERMANN SARAH, Security Analysis of the Object Name Service, available at: http://lasecwww.epfl.ch/~gavoine/download/papers/FabianGS-2005-sptpuc.pdf.

FITZGERALD BRIAN/O'BRIEN DAMIEN/FITZGERALD ANNE, Search Engine Liability for Copyright Infringements, available at: http://eprints.qut.edu.au/7883/1/7883.pdf.

FLOERKEMEIER CHRISTIAN/LANGHEINRICH MARC/FLEISCH ELGAR/MATTERN FRIEDEMANN/SARMA SANJAY E. (eds), The Internet of Things, Berlin/Heidelberg 2008.

FROOMKIN A. MICHAEL, The Death of Privacy?, Stanford Law Review, Vol. 52, 2000, 1461–1543.

GIBBONS LLEWELLYN JOSEPH, No Regulation, Government Regulation, or Self-Regulation: Social Enforcement of Social Contracting for Governance in Cyberspace, Cornell Journal of Law and Public Policy, Vol. 6, 1996–1997, 475–551.

GOLDMAN ERIC, Search Engine Bias and the Demise of Search Engine Utopianism, Yale Journal of Law and Technology, Vol. 8, 2005, 188–200.

GOODHART CHARLES ALBERT ERIC, Regulating the Regulator – An Economist's Perspective on Accountability and Control in: Eilís Ferran/Charles Albert Eric Goodhart (eds), Regulating Financial Services and Markets in the 21st Century, Oxford 2001, 151–164.

GRANT RUTH W./KEOHANE ROBERT O., Accountability and Abuses of Power in World Politics, American Political Science Review, Vol. 99, 2005, 29–43.

GREWLICH KLAUS W., Governance in "cyberspace": access and public interest in global communications, The Hague etc. 1999.

GRIMMELMANN JAMES, The Structure of Search Engine Law, Iowa Law Review, Vol. 93, 2008, 1–63.

GRINGRAS CLIVE, The Laws of the Internet, 2nd edition London 2003.

GRUMMT EBERHARD/MÜLLER MARKUS, Fine-Grained Access Control for EPC Information Services, in: Christian Floerkemeier/Marc Langheinrich/Elgar Fleisch/Friedemann Mattern/Sanjay E. Sarma (eds), The Internet of Things, Berlin/Heidelberg 2008, 35–49.

GUNASEKARA GEHAN, The "Final" Privacy Frontier? Regulating Trans-Border Data Flows, International Journal of Law and Information Technology, Vol. 17, 2009, 147–179.

GÜRSES SEDA F./BERENDT BETTINA/SANTEN THOMAS, Multilateral Security Requirements Analysis for Preserving Privacy in Ubiquitous Environments, in: Bettina Berendt/Ernestina Menasalvas (eds), Workshop on Ubiquitous Knowledge Discovery for Users (UKDU '06), Berlin 2006, 51–64.

HALAVAIS ALEXANDER, Search Engine Society, Cambridge 2009.

HALLER STEPHAN/KARNOUSKOS STAMATIS/SCHROTH CHRISTOPH, The Internet of Things in an Enterprise Context, in: John Domingue/Dieter Fensel/Paolo Traverso (eds), Future Internet – FIS 2008, Berlin 2009, 14–28.

HANDLER DARREN, The Wild Wild West: A Privacy Showdown on the Radio Frequency Identification (RFID) Systems Technological Frontier, Western State University Law Review, Vol. 32, 2005, 199–225.

HAWRYLAK PETER J./MICKLE M.H./CAIN J.T., RFID Tags, in: Lu Yan/Yan Zhang/Laurence T. Yang/Huansheng Ning (eds), The Internet of Things, New York/London 2008, 1–32.

HEALD DAVID, Varieties of Transparency, in: Christopher Hood/David Heald (eds), Transparency. The Key to Better Governance?, Oxford 2006, 25–43.

HILDNER LAURA, Defusing the Threat of RFID: Protecting Consumer Privacy through Technology-Specific Legislation at the State, Harvard Civil Rights – Civil Liberties Law Review, Vol. 41, 2006, 133–176.

HOLZNAGEL BERND/SCHUMACHER PASCAL, Auswirkungen des Grundrechts auf Vertraulichkeit und Integrität informationstechnischer Systeme auf RFID-Chips, Multimedia & Recht, Vol. 12, 2009, 3–8.

HOSEIN GUS, Privacy as Freedom, in: Rikke Frank Jørgensen (ed.), Human Rights in the Global Information Society, Cambridge/Massachusetts 2006, 121–147.

JACOBS SCOTT H., Why Governments Must Work Together, The OECD Observer, Vol. 186, 1994, 13–16.

JAKOBSSON MARKUS/RAMZAN ZULFIKAR, Crimeware: understanding the new attacks and defenses, Upper Saddle River 2008.

JOHNSON DAVID R./POST DAVID G., Law and Borders – The Rise of Law in Cyberspace, Stanford Law Review, Vol. 48, 1996, 1367–1402.

JONES ALISON/SUFRIN BRENDA, EC Competition Law, 3rd edition Oxford 2008.

JUELS ARI, RFID Security and Privacy: A Research Survey, IEEE Journal on Selected Areas in Communications, Vol. 24, 2006, 381–394.

KANG JERRY, Information Privacy in Cyberspace Transactions, Stanford Law Review, Vol. 50, 1998, 1193–1294.

KAUFMAN IAN JAY, The Domain System – Act Now or Regret Later, available at: http://www.ladas.com/Internet/DomainNames/Domain01.html.

KENNEDY DAVID, Five basic rules for the Internet of Things, in: EURESCOM mess@ge, 2/2009, at 7, available at: http://www.eurescom.eu/~pub/about-eurescom/message_2009_02/Eurescom_message_02_2009.pdf.

KEOHANE ROBERT O./NYE JOSEPH S., Power and Interdependence, 3rd edition New York 2001.

KIM KYOUNG HYUN/CHOI EUN YOUNG/LEE SU MI/LEE DONG HOON, Secure EPCglobal Class-1 Gen-2 RFID System Against Security and Privacy Problems, in: Robert Meersman (ed.), On the Move to Meaningful Internet Systems, OTM 2006 Workshops, Berlin 2006, 362–371.

KLEVE PIETER/DEMULDER RICHARD, Privacy protection and the right to information, in: Sylvia Mercado Kierkegaard (ed.), Cyberlaw, Security and Privacy, Beijing 2007, 201–212.

KOH ROBIN/STAAKE THORSTEN, Nutzen von RFID zur Sicherung der Supply Chain der Pharmaindustrie, in: Elgar Fleisch/Friedemann Mattern (eds), Das Internet der Dinge, Berlin/Heidelberg 2005, 161–175.

LANGE STEFAN/SCHIMANK UWE, Governance und gesellschaftliche Integration, in: Stefan Lange/Uwe Schimank (eds), Governance und gesellschaftliche Integration, Wiesbaden 2004, 9–44.

LANGHEINRICH MARC/MATTERN FRIEDEMANN, Wenn der Computer verschwindet, digma 2002, 138–142.

LASTRA ROSA M./SHAMS HEBA, Public Accountability in the Financial Sector, in: Eilis Ferran/Charles Albert Eric Goodhart (eds), Regulating Financial Services and Markets in the 21st Century, Oxford 2001, 165–188.

LEVENE MARK, An Introduction to Search Engines and Web Navigation, Harlow 2006.

LEWICKI FRYDERYK, Progress in the ITU Work Concerning Protection Against Radiation, in: Andrzej Krawczyk/Roman Kubacki/Sławomir Wiak/Carlos Lemos Antunes (eds), Electromagnetic Field, Health and Environment, Amsterdam 2008, 244–248.

MALCOLM JEREMY, Multi-Stakeholder Governance and the Internet Governance Forum, Perth 2008.

MATTERN FRIEDEMANN, Die technische Basis für das Internet der Dinge, in: Elgar Fleisch/Friedemann Mattern (eds), Das Internet der Dinge, Berlin/Heidelberg 2005, 39–66 (MATTERN, Technische Basis).

MATTERN FRIEDEMANN, Ubiquitous Computing: Eine Einführung mit Anmerkungen zu den sozialen und rechtlichen Folgen, in: Jürgen Taeger/Andreas Wiebe (eds), Mobilität, Telematik, Recht, Köln 2005, 1–34 (MATTERN, Ubiquitous Computing).

MAY CHRISTOPHER, The World Intellectual Property Organization, London 2007.

MAYER-SCHÖNBERGER VIKTOR, The Shape of Governance: Analyzing the World of Internet Regulation, Virginia Journal of International Law, Vol. 43, 2003, 605–673.

MAYRHOFER MICHAEL/PLÖCKINGER OLIVER (eds), Aktuelles zum Internet-Recht, Engerwitzdorf 2006.

MEGHABGHAB GEORGE/KANDEL ABRAHAM, Search Engines, Link Analysis and User's Web Behavior, Berlin 2008.

MITCHELL RONALD B., Sources of Transparency: Information Systems in International Regimes, International Studies Quarterly, Vol. 42, 1998, 109–130.

MUELLER MILTON, Securing Internet Freedom: Security, Privacy, and Global Governance, Delft 2008 (MUELLER, Internet Freedom).

MUELLER MILTON, Telecommunications Access in the Age of Electronic Commerce: Toward a Third-Generation Universal Service Policy, Federal Communications Law Journal, Vol. 49, 1997, 655–672 (MUELLER, Telecommunications).

MUGUET FRANCIS, Considerations on Namespace Services for the Networks of Things, EURO-NF WP 3 Workshop on Social-Economics Aspects, June 14–16, 2009, Leipzig, available at: http://www.guarder.net/kleinwaechter/images/euronf/muguet.pdf.

MÜLLER JÜRGEN/HANDY MATTHIAS, RFID als Technik des Ubiquitous Computing – Eine Gefahr für die Privatsphäre?, available at: http://www.imd.uni-rostock.de/veroeff/handy_bamberg05.pdf.

NOBEL PETER, Schweizerisches Finanzmarktrecht, 2nd edition Bern 2004.

NORRIS PIPPA, Digital Divide: Civic Engagement, Information Poverty, and the Internet Worldwide, New York 2001.

PAGE ALAN, Regulating the Regulator – A Lawyer's Perspective on Accountability and Control, in: Eilís Ferran/Charles Albert Eric Goodhart (eds), Regulating Financial Services and Markets in the 21st Century, Oxford 2001, 127–149.

PERRITT HENRY H. JR., The Internet is Changing the Public International Legal System, Kentucky Law Journal, Vol. 88, 1999–2000, 885–955 (PERRITT, Internet).

PERRITT HENRY H. JR., Law and the Information Superhighway, New York 1996 (PERRITT, Information Superhighway).

POSNER RICHARD A., The Right of Privacy, Georgia Law Review, Vol. 12, 1978, 393–422.

POULLET YVES, The Directive 95/46/EC: Ten years after, Computer Law and Security Report, 2006, 206–217.

PREUVENEERS DAVY/BERBERS YOLANDE, Internet of Things: A Context-Awareness Perspective, in: Lu Yan/Yan Zhang/Laurence T. Yang/Huansheng Ning (eds), The Internet of Things, New York/London 2008, 287–307.

PRIBRAM KARL, Geschichte des öknomischen Denkens, Volume I, Frankfurt am Main 1992.

RAUSTIALA KAL, The Architecture of International Cooperation: Transgovernmental Networks and the Future of International Law, Virginia Journal of International Law, Vol. 43, 2002, 1–92.

REIDENBERG JOEL R., Resolving Conflicting International Data Privacy Rules in Cyberspace, Stanford Law Review, Vol. 52, 2000, 1315–1371.

REINICKE WOLFGANG H., Global Public Policy, Foreign Affairs, Vol. 76, 1997, 127–138.

RUGGIE JOHN GERARD, Reconstituting the Global Public Domain – Issues, Actors and Practices, European Journal of International Relations, 2004, 499–531.

SAKAMURA KEN, Ubiquitous ID Technologies 2009, available at: http://www.uidcenter.org/pdf/UID910-W001-090511_en.pdf.

SAMUELSON PAMELA, Privacy as Intellectual Property?, Stanford Law Review, Vol. 52, 2000, 1125–1173.

SANTUCCI GERALD, Paper for the International Conference on Future Trends of the Internet, From Internet of Data to Internet of Things, available at: ftp://ftp.cordis.europa.eu/pub/fp7/ ict/docs/enet/20090128-speech-iot-conference-lux_en.pdf.

SCHERER JOACHIM (ed.), Telecommunication Laws in Europe, 5th edition Haywards Heath 2005.

SCHMID BEAT F., Digitalisierte Wirtschaft: Praktisch kein Stein bleibt auf dem anderen, in: Albert Kündig/Danielle Bütschi (eds), Die Verselbständigung des Computers, Zurich 2008, 99–116 (SCHMID, Digitalisierte Wirtschaft).

SCHMID VIOLA, Radio Frequency Identification Law Beyond 2007, in: Christian Floerkemeier/Marc/Langheinrich/Elgar Fleisch/Friedemann Mattern/Sanjay E. Sarma (eds), The Internet of Things, Berlin/Heidelberg 2008, 196–213 (SCHMID, Radio Frequency Identification).

SCHULZ ROBERT, Der Zugang zum "blanken Draht" im Telekommunikationsrecht: Wettbewerb im Netz oder Wettbewerb zwischen Netzen?, Munich 2001.

SHIH DONG-HER/SUN PO-LING/LIN BINSHAN, Securing industry-wide EPCglobal Network with WS-Security, Industrial Management and Data Services, Vol. 105, 2005, 972–996.

SINGH J.P., Negotiation and the Global Information Economy, Cambridge/Mass. 2009.

SLAUGHTER ANNE-MARIE, A New World Order, Princeton/Oxford 2004.

SMITH ADAM, An Inquiry into the Nature and Causes of the Wealth of Nations, edited by Edwin Cannan, Chicago 1976.

SMITH GRAHAM J.H., Internet Law and Regulation, 3rd edition London 2002.

STAVROULAKIS PETER (ed.), Reliability, Survivability and Quality of Large Scale Telecommunication Systems, Chichester 2003.

STÖGMÜLLER THOMAS, Vertraulichkeit und Integrität informationstechnischer Systeme im Unternehmen, Computer & Recht, 2008, 435–439.

SUNSTEIN CASS R., Republic.com, Princeton 2001 (SUNSTEIN, Republic.com).

SUNSTEIN CASS R., Deliberative Trouble? Why Groups go to Extremes, Yale Law Journal, Vol. 110, 2000, pp. 71–119 (SUNSTEIN, Deliberative Trouble).

SYKES ALAN O., Comparative Advantage and the Normative Economics of International Trade Policy, Journal of International Economic Law, Vol. 1, 1998, 49–82.

TEGGE ANDREAS, Die Internationale Telekommunikations-Union, Baden-Baden 1994.

THÜRER DANIEL, Völkerrecht als Fortschritt und Chance, Zurich/St. Gallen 2009.

TRACHTMAN JOEL P., The Domain of WTO Dispute Resolution, available at: http://papers.ssrn.com/sol3/papers.cfm?abstract_id=149348.

TWOMEY PAUL, Effect of Multilingualism on the Internet, NSF/OECD Workshop, January 31, 2007, available at: http://www.oecd.org/dataoecd/12/18/38014552.pdf.

VAN DER TOGT REMKO/VAN LIESHOUT ERIK JAN/HENSBROEK REINOUT/BEINAT E./BINNEKADE J.M./BAKKER P.J.M., Electromagnetic Interference From Radio Frequency Identification Inducing Potentially Hazardous Incidents in Critical Care Medical Equipment, JAMA Vol. 24(299), 2008, 2884–2890.

WARREN SAMUEL D./BRANDEIS LOUIS D., The Right to Privacy, Harvard Law Review, Vol. 4, 1890, 193–220.

WEBER ROLF H., Internet of Things – New Security and Privacy Challenges, Computer Law & Security Report, forthcoming January 2010 (WEBER, Security and Privacy).

WEBER ROLF H., Internet of Things – Need for a New Legal Environment?, Computer Law & Security Report, Vol. 25, 2009, 522–527 (WEBER, Legal Environment).

WEBER ROLF H., Internet Corporation for Assigned Names and Numbers (ICANN), in: Christian Tietje/Alan Brouder (eds), Handbook of Transnational Economic Governance Regimes, Leiden 2009, 603–619 (WEBER, ICANN).

WEBER ROLF H., Shaping Internet Governance: Regulatory Challenges, Zurich 2009 (WEBER, Internet Governance).

WEBER ROLF H., Transparency and the Governance of the Internet, Computer Law & Security Report, Vol. 24, 2008, 342–342 (WEBER, Transparency).

WEBER ROLF H., Grundrecht auf Gewährleistung der Vertraulichkeit und Integrität, digma, 2008, 94–97 (WEBER, Vertraulichkeit und Integrität).

WEBER ROLF H., Looking ahead: more harmonization in the domain name system?, International Journal for Intercultural Information Management, Vol. 1, 2007, 74–84 (WEBER, More harmonization in the DNS).

WEBER ROLF H., Selbstregulierung und Selbstorganisation bei den elektronischen Medien, Medialex 2004, 211–217 (WEBER, Selbstregulierung und Selbstorganisation).

WEBER ROLF H., Towards a Legal Framework for the Information Society, Zurich 2003 (WEBER, Information Society).

WEBER ROLF H., Rechtsfragen rund um Suchmaschinen, Zurich 2003 (WEBER, Suchmaschinen).

WEBER ROLF H., Regulatory Models for the Online World, Zurich 2002 (WEBER, Regulatory Models).

WEBER ROLF H./DARBELLAY ALINE, Vers une evolution des marches financiers au service de la protection de l'environnement, in: Rita Trigo Trindade/Henry Peter/Christian Bovet (eds), Economie Environnement Ethique, de la responsabilité sociale et sociétale, Liber Amicorum Anne Petitpierre-Sauvain, Geneva/Basel/Zurich 2009, 401–407.

WEBER ROLF H./GROSZ MIRINA, Internet Governance – From Vague Ideas to Realistic Implementation, Medialex 2007, 119–135 (WEBER/GROSZ, Vague Ideas)

WEBER ROLF H./MENOUD VALÉRIE, The Information Society and the Digital Divide, Legal Strategies to Finance Global Access, Zurich/Basel/Geneva 2008 (WEBER/MENOUD, Digital Divide).

WEBER ROLF H./MENOUD VALÉRIE, The Digital Solidarity Clause – An Analysis in the Light of Contract, Public Procurement and Competition Law, in: Peter Gauch/Franz Werro/Pascal Pichonnaz (eds), Mélanges en l'honneur de Pierre Tercier, Zurich/Basel/Geneva 2008, 471–494 (WEBER/MENOUD, Digital Solidarity Clause).

WEBER ROLF H./WEBER ROMANA, Inclusion of the Civil Society in the Governance of the Internet, Can Lessons be Drawn from the Environmental Legal Framework?, Computer Law Review International (CRi) 2009, 9–15 (WEBER/WEBER, Civil Society).

WEBER ROLF H./WEBER ROMANA, International ordre public for terrorism-related Internet content?, Humboldt Forum Recht, Vol. 4, 2009, 52–73 (WEBER/WEBER, ordre public).

WEBER ROLF H./WILLI ANNETTE, IT-Sicherheit und Recht, Zurich 2006.

WHISH RICHARD, Competition Law, 6th edition Oxford 2009.

WOLLING JENS, Suchmaschinen – Gatekeeper im Internet, Medienwirtschaft 2/2002, 15–23.

YAN LU/ZHANG YAN/YANG LAURENCE T./NING HUANSHENG (eds), The Internet of Things, New York/London 2008.

YU PETER K., Bridging the Digital Divide: Equality in the Information Age, Cardozo Arts & Entertainment Law Journal, Vol. 20, 2002, 1–52.

Weblinks have been last checked on November 1, 2009.

Materials

The following documents listed here will not be cited anew in the footnotes

International Organizations:

International Telecommunication Union (ITU), Internet of Things, available at: http://www.itu.int/osg/spu/publications/internetofthings/InternetofThings_summary.pdf.

Tunis Agenda for the Information Society, November 2005, available at: http://www.itu.int/wsis/docs2/tunis/off/6rev1.html.

European Union (EU):

EU Commission, Internet of Things, Strategic Research Roadmap, September 15, 2009, available at: http://ec.europa.eu/information_society/policy/rfid/documents/in_cerp. pdf.

EU Commission Staff Working Document, Future Networks and the Internet – Early Challenges regarding the "Internet of Things", available at: http://ec.europa.eu/information_society/eeurope/i2010/docs/future_internet/swp_internet_things.pdf.

EU Communication, Internet of Things – An action plan for Europe, June 18, 2009, COM (2009) 278 final.

EU Commission Recommendation on the implementation of privacy and data protection principles in applications supported by radio-frequency identification, May 12, 2009, C(2009) 3200 final, available at: http://ec.europa.eu/information_society/policy/rfid/documents/recommendationonrfid2009.pdf.

EU Directive 2002/58/EC of the European Parliament and of the Council of July 12, 2002 concerning the processing of personal data and the protection of privacy in the electronic communications sector, OJ L 201/37.

EC Directive 1999/5/EC of the European Parliament and of the Council of March 9, 1999 on radio equipment and telecommunications terminal equipment and the mutual recognition of their conformity, OJ L 91/10.

EC Directive 95/46/EC of the European Parliament and of the Council of October 24, 1995 on the protection of individuals with regard to the processing of personal data and on the free movement of such data, OJ L 281/31.

State Directions:

Deutsches Bundesministerium für Wirtschaft und Technologie, Dokumentation Nr. 581, Internet der Dinge, available at: http://www.vdivde-it.de/publikationen/dokumente/doku-581-internet-der-dinge.pdf.

Non-Governmental Organizations:

Afilias, White Paper on "Finding your Way in the Internet of Things", September 2008, available at: http://www.afilias.info/webfm_send/11.

Amcham EU, Response to "Internet of Things" Public Consultation, available at: http://www.eucommittee.be/Pops/2008/DEC_Internet%20of%20Things%2028112008.pdf.

CASAGRAS, Final Report, RFID and the Inclusive Model for the Internet of Things, EU Project Number 216803.

EuroCommerce, Position Paper, November 28, 2008, available at: http://ec.europa.eu/information_society/policy/rfid/documents/c_eurocommerce.pdf.

European Technology Platform on Smart Systems Integration (EPoSS), Internet of Things in 2020, available at: http://www.iot-visitthefuture.eu/fileadmin/documents/researchforeurope/270808_IoT_in_2020_Workshop_Report_V1–1.pdf.

Joint ANEC/BEUC answer to the consultation, November 27, 2008, available at: http://ec.europa.eu/information_society/policy/rfid/documents/c_anec_beuc.pdf.

NIST Guidelines for Securing Radio Frequency Identification Systems 4–4 (2007), available at: http://csrc.nist.gov/publications/nistpubs/800–98/SP800–98_RFID-2007.pdf.

EPCglobal:

EPCglobal, Response to the EU Commission Staff Working Document: Future Networks and the Internet – Early Challenges regarding the "Internet of Things", available at: http://ec.europa.eu/information_society/policy/rfid/documents/c_epcglobal.pdf.

EPCglobal, Object Naming Service (ONS) Version 1.0.1, available at: http://www.epcglobalinc.org/standards/ons/ons_1_0_1-standard-20080529.pdf.

Weblinks have been last checked on November 1, 2009.

Abbreviations

Amcham EU	American Chamber of Commerce to the European Union
ANEC	European Association for the Coordination of Consumer Representation in Standardization
Art.	Article
ASCII	American Standard Code for Information Interchange
BEUC	European Consumer's Organization
ccTLD	country code Top-Level Domain
CDM	Collaborative Decision Making
DHT	Distributed Hash Tables
DNS	Domain Name System
DNSSEC	DNS Security Extensions
DSF	Digital Solidarity Fund
EC	European Community
ECHR	European Convention on Human Rights
ed./eds.	editor/editors
e.g.	for example
EMS	Electromagnetic Fields
EPC	Electronic Product Code
EPCIS	Electronic Product Code Information Services
EPoSS	European Technology Platform on Smart Systems Integration
EU	European Union
FATF	Financial Action Task Force
GHz	Gigahertz
GPS	Global Positioning System
GRIFS	Global RFID Interoperability Forum for Standards
gTLD	generic Top-Level Domain
ICANN	Internet Corporation for Assigned Names and Numbers
ICCPR	International Covenant on Civil and Political Rights
ICNIRP	International Commission on Non-Ionizing Radiation Protection
ICC	International Criminal Court
IDN	Internationalized Domain Name
i.e.	that is; Latin abbreviation for "id est"
IEC	International Electrotechnical Commission
IETF	Internet Engineering Task Force
ILC	International Law Commission
IGF	Internet Governance Forum
IoT	Internet of Things
IP	Internet Protocol
ISP	Internet Service Provider

IT	Information Technology
ITU	International Telecommunication Union
ISO	International Organization for Standardization
ISP	Internet Service Provider
kHz	Kilohertz
MONS	Multipolar Object Naming Service
MoU	Memorandum of Understanding
NGO	Non-governmental Organization
No.	Number
OECD	Organization for Economic Cooperation and Development
OFCOM	Federal Office for Communication
OIDA	Object-Information Distribution Architecture
ONS	Object Naming Service
para./paras.	paragraph/paragraphs
PET	Privacy Enhancing Technologies
PIA	Private Impact Assessment
PIR	Private Information Retrieval
PKI	Public Key Infrastructure
P2P	Peer-to-Peer Systems
P3P	Platform for Privacy Preferences
RFC	Request for Comments
RFID	Radio-Frequency Identification
RRs	Resource Records
SOA	Service Oriented Architecture
SR	Systematische Sammlung des (Schweizerischen) Bundesrechts
TLD	Top-level Domain
TLS	Transport Layer Security
UDHR	Universal Declaration of Human Rights
UN	United Nations
UNECE	United Nations Economic Commission for Europe
UNEP	United Nations Environment Program
URI	Uniform Resource Identifier
US	United States
USD	United States Dollars
Vol.	Volume
VPN	Virtual Private Networks
WIPO	World Intellectual Property Organization
WSIS	World Summit on the Information Society
WTO	World Trade Organization
W3C	World Wide Web Consortium

I. Introduction

A. Internet of Things: Notion

The Internet of Things (IoT)[1] is an emerging global Internet-based information architecture facilitating the exchange of goods and services.[2] The IoT has the purpose of providing an IT-infrastructure facilitating the exchange of "things" in a secure and reliable manner, i.e. its function is to overcome the gap between objects in the physical world and their representation in information systems.[3] The IoT will serve to increase transparency and enhance the efficiency of global supply chain networks.[4]

HALLER/KARNOUSKOS/SCHROTH define the IoT as "a world where physical objects are seamlessly integrated into the information network, and where the physical objects can become active participants in business processes. Services are available to interact with these 'smart objects' over the Internet, query their state and any information associated with them, taking into account security and privacy issues."[5]

Extending the initial application scope, the IoT might also serve as backbone for ubiquitous computing, enabling smart environments to recognize and identify objects, and retrieve information from the Internet to facilitate their adaptive functionality.[6]

Through the IoT, everyday objects (such as cars, refrigerators, umbrellas, etc. as well as more advanced, computer and information services) will be able to interact and communicate.[7] „Things" do not have to be products of higher technology – any one of the around 50,000 billion objects existing on earth can be introduced in the IoT.[8]

Many good examples have been provided. They include cars warning other cars of traffic jams, a cell phone reminding a person when it was last left next to the

1 The term "IoT" has been "invented" by KEVIN ASHTON in a presentation in 1998 (see SANTUCCI, 2).

2 For a general overview see WEBER, Legal Environment, 522–523.

3 HALLER/KARNOUSKOS/SCHROTH, 15.

4 FABIAN, 1.

5 HALLER/KARNOUSKOS/SCHROTH, 15.

6 See in general FABIAN, 1.

7 PREUVENEERS/BERBERS, 288.

8 SANTUCCI, 3–4.

R.H. Weber and R. Weber, *Internet of Things*, DOI 10.1007/978-3-642-11710-7_1,

keys, a wastebin inquiring its contents about their recicability, or a medicine cabinet checking the storage life of the medications in it.[9]

The question has been raised why the IoT does not already exist, considering that the Internet, mobile devices and data carriers exist for quite some time. The answer thereto lies in the fact that persons do not communicate with the tools being already available to their possible extent. Barcodes, GPS, RFID etc. are closed-loop systems that are not yet bound together, but that are systems standing alone.[10]

B. Technicity of the Internet of Things

The IoT is a very complex platform for the connection of things based on objects being tagged for their identification, but also sensors,[11] actuating elements and other technologies. In this book, the focus is put on the identification of things, which is the most important (while not the only) aspect[12] of the IoT as far as the involvement of businesses is concerned.

1. Technical Elements

1.1 Radio-Frequency Identification (RFID)

a) RFID in General

From a technical point of view, the architecture of the IoT is based on data communication tools, primarily RFID-tagged items (Radio-Frequency Identification). RFID is a technology used to identify, track and locate assets. The RFID technique has been known since at least the Second World War[13] and has, up to now, been used primarily in new civil application fields.[14] This technology is gradually replacing the existing bar-codes, not requiring any contact with objects.[15] As the number of tags produced increases, it is expected their price will decrease.

---

9 Mattern, Ubiquitous Computing, 17.

10 Oral statement of Bert Moore, AIM, Director, Communications and Media Relations at the CASAGRAS Conference in London on October 6–7, 2009.

11 The use of sensors in the IoT is discussed in chapter V.D. with regard to environmental concerns.

12 Other aspects are the autonomous operation of objects or the communication between things.

13 Shih/Sun/Lin, 973.

14 Such as animal or human identification, anti-counterfeiting, access control and payment; Fabian, 1–2.

15 Usually, RFID tags can be read from about 20 meters away.

RFID is a technology for the automatic identification of objects through wireless radio waves. In general, RFID systems consist of two components: a transponder (RFID tag or chip), attached to the object and serving as data carrier, and a registration device reading the data in the transponder.[16] RFID tags can either be passive (not possessing a battery), active (with an integrated battery including an active transmitter and receiver), or semi-passive (with battery but no transmitter).[17]

While RFID seems to be the technology referred to most often when considering the architecture of the IoT, one has to keep in mind that it is not the only technology available. Other tools such as Near Field Communication Technologies,[18] wireless sensors, 2D barcodes or inks with nano-particles could also be used instead of RFID.[19] The employment of other technologies than RFID for the IoT has also been emphasized in responses to the European Commission regarding a working document on the challenges of the IoT.[20]

16 Weber/Willi, 245–246; Mattern, Technische Basis, 55–57; Arioli/Thalmann, 550; see also Kim/Choi/Lee/Lee, 364; Müller/Handy, 3.

17 For RFID tags see Benghozi/Bureau/Massit-Folléa, 95; Hawrylak/Mickle/Cain; Juels, 382.

18 From a technical point of view, Near Field Communication Technologies could be classified as a kind of RFID because they are partly based on the same standards. However, from a political point of view, in particular representatives of Near Field Communication Technologies are opposed to that view in order to prevent the partly negative connotations of RFID with regard to privacy to be transfered to Near Field Communication Technologies.

19 Amcham EU, 4; EPCglobal, Response to the EU Commission Staff Working Document, 2–4; see also Mattern, Techische Basis, 49–50.

20 Amcham EU, 4; EPCglobal, Response to the EU Commission Staff Working Document, 2–4.

The basic RFID Device and Process Architecture is illustrated in the following graph:[21]

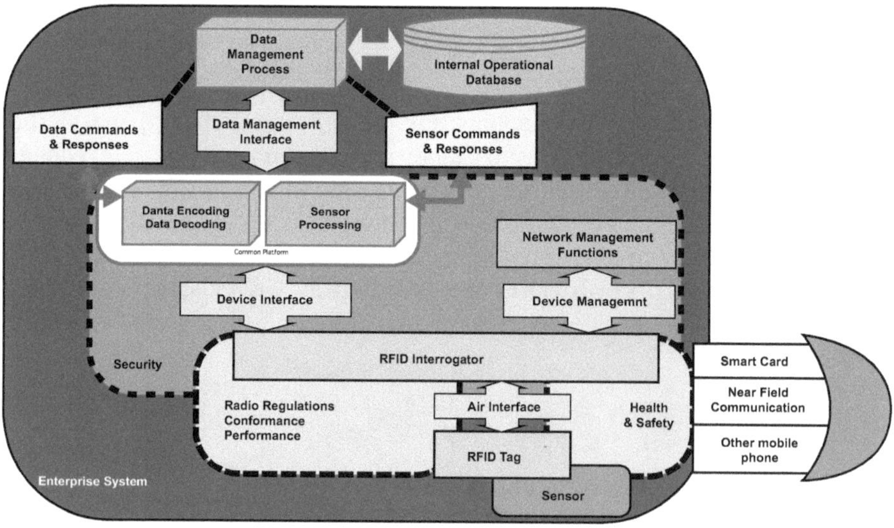

b) Global RFID Interoperability Forum for Standards (GRIFS)

The Global RFID Interoperability Forum for Standards (GRIFS) is an EU project lasting from January 2008 to December 2009. The GRIFS is engaged in RFID standardization for physical items. It documents the development of standards, establishes liaisons of existing standards and, most importantly, provides for a forum for standards (this forum should continue even after the end of the project in December 2009).[22]

In May 2009, a Memorandum of Understanding (MoU) was effectively launched between key stakeholders (IEC, ISO, ITU and UNECE). This MoU has been established for the facilitation of standards. It does not constitute a change to the existing standards development process and decisions have to be taken by consensus.[23]

---

21 Graph taken over from a presentation of PAUL CHARTIER at the CASAGRAS Conference in London on October 6–7, 2009.

22 See http://www.grifs-project.eu/index.php/home/en/.

23 GRIFS Memorandum of Understanding, Version 1.1, August 26, 2009, available at: http://www.grifs-project.eu/data/File/GRIFS_MoU_Version1%201.pdf.

1.2 Electronic Product Code (EPC)

The most popular industry proposal for the new IT-infrastructure of the IoT is based on an Electronic Product Code (EPC), introduced by EPCglobal[24] and GS1.[25] EPCglobal is a consortium focused on developing and establishing global standards for RFID, EPC, and the EPCglobal Network.[26]

The EPC is made up of a header, which determines the kind of EPC and how to interpret the other parts of the EPC.[27] Most often, the actual EPC consists of an EPC Manager Number, an Object Class Code and a Serial Number (or a subset thereof).[28] EPCs are unique numbers[29] encoded in an inexpensive RFID tag.[30] EPC tags can store up to 256 bits.[31] Physical objects consequently carry these RFID tags with the EPCs.[32]

While EPCs allow for users to verify the integrity of the ordered object,[33] a "tracking and tracing" of things on their way from the sender to the recipient is not possible. Such result could only be achieved by the sender delivering a file to the recipient including all information on the delivery before sending off the object.[34]

The EPC Network allows many parties to register any information for the objects they are concerned with, thereby creating a process to openly exchange product-related information.[35] This information can consist of EPC-encoded sensor data, historical data or business context.[36] Furthermore, the infrastructure is able to offer and query EPC Information Services (EPCIS) both locally and remotely to subscribers.[37]

---

24 EPCglobal is a joint venture of GS1 U.S. (formerly Uniform Code Council) and GS1 (formerly EAN International).

25 See http.//www.epcglobalinc.org.

26 FABIAN, 30.

27 See EPCglobal, EPC Tag Data Standards, Version 1.4, available at: http://www.epcglobal inc.org/standards/tds/tds_1_4-standard-20080611.pdf.

28 EPCglobal, Object Naming Service (ONS) Version 1.0.1, Appendix A.

29 For the numbers of EPCs that can be generated without duplicates see FABIAN, 94–96.

30 EPCglobal, Object Naming Service (ONS) Version 1.0.1, para 4.

31 DALAL, 487.

32 FABIAN/GÜNTHER/SPIEKERMANN, 1.

33 For security and privacy of the IoT see also below III.

34 KOH/STAAKE, 17.

35 FABIAN/GÜNTHER/SPIEKERMANN, 1.

36 FABIAN/GÜNTHER, Security Challenges, 122.

37 See FABIAN, 30–31; to the details of the service orientation and the context-aware computing see PREUVENEERS/BERBERS, 296–299.

1.3 Object Naming Service (ONS)

a) ONS in General

The Object Naming Service (ONS) is a service containing the network addresses of services. Each service available on the ONS contains data about EPCs. Instead of saving all the information on an RFID tag, a supply of the information by distributed servers on the Internet is achievable through linking and cross-linking with the help of the ONS.[38] The ONS does not contain actual data about EPCs, but can return a list of network accessible endpoints that pertain to the EPC in question.[39] The first ONS was introduced by the (private) company VeriSign, the first European ONS was established by France in 2009.

The ONS is authoritative (linking metadata and services) in the sense that the entity having – centralized – change control over the information about the EPC is the same entity that assigned the EPC to the concerned item.[40]

Using the ONS, the architecture can also serve as a backbone for ubiquitous computing, enabling smart environments to recognize and identify objects, and receive information from the Internet to facilitate their adaptive functionality.[41] The practical operation of the central ONS root has been outsourced to VeriSign, a provider of Internet infrastructure services.

b) ONS and DNS Heritage

The ONS is based on the well-known Domain Name System (DNS), i.e. the DNS-based ONS as hierarchical tree-like architecture[42] locates the information sources relevant for a given object. Technically, in order to use the DNS to find information about an item, the item's EPC must be converted into a format that the DNS can understand, which is the typical, "dot" delimited, left to right form of all domain names.[43] In practice, the EPC in the binary form is forwarded to a middleware system. This system converts the EPC to its Uniform Resource Identifier (URI) in order to locate the relevant EPCIS for the searched product. The ONS finally translates the URI into a domain name according a well-defined procedure.[44]

38 Fabian, 33.
39 Weber, Legal Environment, 523.
40 EPCglobal, Object Naming Service (ONS) Version 1.0.1, para 4.2.
41 Fabian, 1.
42 Fabian, 33.
43 EPCglobal, Object Naming Service (ONS) Version 1.0.1, para 5.2.
44 Fabian/Günther/Spiekermann, 1.

There are two options that need to be explored. Firstly, the IoT could have an exclusive generic Top-Level Domain (gTLD), e.g. the address .iot. In the Internet, seven gTLDs were created in the beginning: .com for commercial activities, .org for organizations, and .net for networks as three universal top-level domains; .gov for governments, .edu for universities, and .mil for military as three gTLDs for use in the US only, and .int for intergovernmental treaty organizations.[45] In the following, the list of gTLDs was enlarged. In particular, each country was given its own name according to the so-called country code Top-Level Domain (ccTLD) such as .de for Germany, .ch for Switzerland, .uk for the United Kingdom and .us for the US.[46] On November 15, 2000, the ICANN passed a resolution to introduce seven new gTLDs.[47] Since then, six more gTLDS have been introduced.[48] However, these extensions have lead to confusion regarding the gTLDs themselves as well as their corresponding dispute resolution policies.[49]

With regard to the IoT, commercial pressure against the introduction of an .iot address may emerge from the business sector, which wants to retain e.g. an address .com.

Furthermore, gTLDs relating to a sector and for sector-specific identifiers, resolvers and discovery services could be employed (e.g. the address .aero for organizations in the air transportation sector).[50]

Since EPC is encoded into a syntactically correct domain name and then used within the existing DNS infrastructure, the ONS can be considered as subset of the DNS.[51] For this reason, however, the ONS will also inherit all of the well-documented DNS weaknesses, such as the limited redundancy in practical implementations and the creation of single points of failure.[52]

---

45 For the naming system see BYGRAVE/SCHIAVETTA/THUNEM/LANGE/PHILLIPS.

46 WEBER, ICANN, 604; for ccTLD governance see BYGRAVE/SCHIAVETTA/THUNEM/LANGE/PHILLIPS, 156–159.

47 The addresses .aero for the air-transport industry, .biz for business, .coop for cooperatives, .info for unrestricted use, .museum for museums, .name for registration by individuals and .pro for registration by accountants, lawyers, physicians and the like.

48 The addresses .asia for the Asian community, .cat for the Catalan linguistics and cultural community, .jobs for the international community of human resource managers, .mobi for the mobile content providers and users community, .tel for e-communications address/numbers information and .travel for the travel and tourism community; for an overview of all current gTLDs see BYGRAVE/SCHIAVETTA/THUNEM/LANGE/PHILLIPS, 149.

49 KAUFMAN, 4–6.

50 CASAGRAS, 41.

51 For similarities and differences of the ONS and the DNS see WEBER, Legal Environment, 523.

52 For more details see WEBER, Legal Environment, 523; FABIAN/GÜNTHER, Distributed ONS, 1224.

The ONS and the DNS have the following similarities:

- *Structure*: Based on the distributed DNS-tree, both the ONS and the DNS are grounded on the same database structure.
- *Service architecture*: Both the ONS and DNS use the architectural user-server model and the same Internet communication protocols.

The following differences are given between the ONS and the DNS:

- *Standardization processes and bodies*: The ONS uses the standards development process by EPCglobal, a user driven standards process for the development of technical standards, whereas DNS applies the RFC (Requests for Comments) series, a standardization process developed and published by the Internet Engineering Task Force (IETF).
- *Naming schemes*: The domain names in the DNS usually consist of two or more alphanumeric parts (labels) with only a few technical limits, e.g. each label can contain up to 63 octets, but the whole domain name may not exceed 255 octets. The ONS uses the Tag Data Standard, a deterministic choice based on the EPC structure.[53]
- *Use models*: The DNS is based on an extensible and multi-purpose Internet-based public infrastructure; the ONS uses a private infrastructure that is specific to RFID-related business activities/partners.

c) Introduction of Multiple DNS Classes

MUGUET proposes to use various DNS classes, each being an autonomous namespace with its own root servers and its own governance.[54] This approach allows for decentralized security systems related to each DNS class, offering participants commercial and political independence.[55]

The operation of the IoT could go through several classes in order to present an independent and interoperable IoT. Classes may be established according to the International Classification of Trademarks[56] encompassing 45 classes. This Classification was introduced in the Internet because it was deemed necessary to establish harmonized rules governing domain names. The Nice Classification is based upon the respective multilateral treaty, distinguishing between a broad variety of goods and services. Therefore, the classes are suitable to serve as code

53 FABIAN, 37.

54 MUGUET, 3.

55 MUGUET, 4.

56 According to the Nice Agreement Concerning the International Classification of Goods and Services for the Purposes of the Registration of Marks of June 15, 1957.

rules.[57] In the IoT, each label would have a domain name in a DNS class related to its trademark class. Such an approach would not only provide for decentralized power, but also represent a tool against counterfeiting.[58]

While MUGUET's proposal allows for decentralized power as well as potentially increased security and product verification, the classification of objects into various classes could, in practice, pose a major logistical problem and require extensive resources. The introduction of classes increases the complexity of the IoT and therefore makes it more exposed to failures. Furthermore, the proposal still operates with only one root, which does not alleviate the problem of a "single point of failure".

1.4 EPC Discovery Service

The EPC Discovery Services are another locator of EPC-related data. Unlike ONS, however, an EPC Discovery Services may not only contain pointers to the entity that originally assigned the EPC code, but any entity. Thus, EPC Discovery Services are not universally authoritative for the data they have about an EPC. Nevertheless, it is anticipated that various EPC Discovery-Services, in a competitive relationship, will be established, some of them with a scope limited e.g. geographically or according to objects.[59]

1.5 Graphic Overview

The finding of information using an RFID tagged object can – in very simple terms – be demonstrated in a graph:

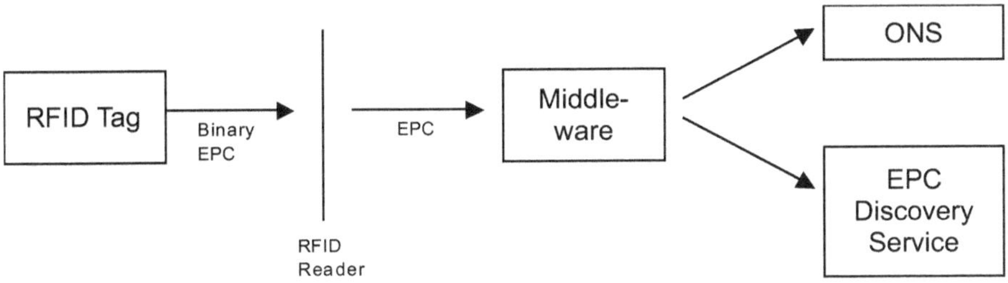

57 WEBER, More harmonization in the DNS, 454–455.
58 MUGUET, 5.
59 EPCglobal, Object Naming Service (ONS) Version 1.0.1, para 4.2.

2. Decentralized and Interoperable Internet of Things

2.1 Introduction

As the IoT is based on the Internet, the framework of the Internet shall be examined and serve as a basis of understanding for the establishment of the IoT. The currently used Internet model, maintained by the Internet Corporation of Assigned Names and Numbers (ICANN), a US-domiciled private entity, is hierarchically structured as a single authoritative root with complete interoperability based on common standards.[60] In this context, the question whether a single- or a multi-root architecture would be preferable merits further elaboration.

The fact that the concentration of the *de jure* control over the root name space is in the hands of a single non-governmental entity is subject to constant criticism,[61] since, for example, a unique root does not meet geopolitical concerns. Therefore, structural changes are of fundamental importance. Furthermore, a unipolar ONS could be controlled or blocked by a single country or a group of countries based on political or economic reasons.[62] Even if no single server would contain the complete ONS directory and if each server would be responsible for one or more domains but no two servers for the same domain, a fully centralized root system does not seem to be appropriate.[63]

Therefore, an independently managed decentralized multiple-root system being interoperable and covering data in a distributed way needs to be developed for the future IoT, although multiple identifier authorities imply a significant and sustained effort of global cooperation[64]. The need therefore can be slightly limited through the introduction of common standards that apply to all identifier authorities. Nevertheless, continuous dialogue between all authorities regarding current events and possible improvements of the system is indispensable to preserve the globality and uniformity of the IoT.

Nevertheless, the implementation of a multi-root system does not exclude that a close cooperation between EPCglobal/GS1 and the domain name registries is applied; by sharing experiences and by putting together combined efforts it should be possible to realize better and more stable solutions. Furthermore, a multipolar

60 For information about the ICANN see Weber, ICANN, 603–619.

61 See Fabian, 50.

62 Evdokimov/Fabian/Günther, 4–5.

63 In general see Weber, Internet Governance, 61–63; for the IoT context see Benhamou, Governance Perspective, 268; see also Fabian, 38–39.

64 Santucci, 18.

ONS (MONS) allows for the distribution of control between the participating parties.[65]

2.2 Replicated Multipolar ONS

One possible scenario of replicated MONS consists of an ONS root running on six locally distributed servers. These servers would all be operated by the company VeriSign; this concept herewith differs from the existing DNS where root name servers are operated by various entities.

A second setting would be to replicate the ONS root between various independent servers. These servers would have to synchronize the instances of the root ONS, which could be achieved by EPCglobal distributing a master copy. In order to delimit the number of incoming requests, each server would be responsible to cover a certain area of the Internet Protocol (IP) topology and respond only to requests originating from that area. These individual servers can consequently provide their services in parallel to the root ONS operated by VeriSign.

Both scenarios of the multiple replicated ONS would enhance availability. However, the establishment of an according structure might not be globally accessible due to a high load of data and result in an unstructured patchwork of areas with ONS root redundancy.[66]

2.3 Regional Multipolar ONS

In particular European scholars call for a root system on a regional basis, representing the whole of the Internet community within the organizational structures. Correspondingly, democratic legitimacy[67] is only considered as being achievable through various root systems.[68]

Evdokimov/Fabian/Günther have addressed the possibility of regional MONS. Regional MONS would allow reducing the size of the root zone file and the frequency of its updates. The authoritative region for membership could be determined by a company's registration address or the address of the regional GS1 department that issued the company prefix. While regional MONS are a promising approach, the delegation of queries from one regional ONS to another constitutes an additional resolution step. This step asks for an extension of the existing EPC scheme. To encounter this problem, the first three digits of the company pre-

65 Evdokimov/Fabian/Günther, 7.

66 Evdokimov/Fabian/Günther, 7–9.

67 See below IV.B.

68 Benhamou, Governance Perspective, 269.

fix that identify the country could be used, or a regional prefix would need to be established. As a region's MONS root will be perceived as the root of the whole hierarchy by a resolver, the structure of regional MONS can be called a relative hierarchy, allowing for the implementation of the regional MONS within the DNS. In addition, this system has the advantage that each region could determine its own resolution architectures for subsystems below the root zone, thereby allowing for a modularity of the ONS.[69]

The establishment of regional roots has also been proposed by the French government to the EU in 2008. The French government wanted the EU to establish its own root for the Internet of Things, as an alternative to the ONS created by EPCglobal. The technology of the proposed root would not differentiate from the ONS – both systems rely on the DNS – but would have a different registry and use the top level domain ".eu" instead of ".com". In the opinion of the French government, the Internet of the future asks for areas administered by regions (and not globally).[70]

2.4 Referral Systems

Afilias, a large provider of global domain name registry services supporting over 14 million domains across 15 top level domains[71], published a White Paper on "Finding your Way in the Internet of Things" in September 2008. Afilias therein submits an architectural approach to ONS for creating a decentralized and interoperable IoT root system focusing on five main issues,[72] namely identifier collusions, backward compatibility, unilateral control authority, assurance of practicality, openness to competition in the provision of services and setting of priorities towards trust/security.[73]

In practice, identifier authorities could set up referral systems under any top level domain, thereby establishing ONS operations. To satisfy the requirement of interoperability, these identifier authorities would need to cooperate and coordinate the look up of their identifiers in global supply chains.[74]

In the EPC that has been transformed into a DNS format, a "dot" constitutes a delegation step, and thus a pointer to a subsequent zone.[75] Accordingly, the Inter-

69 EVDOKIMOV/FABIAN/GÜNTHTER, 9–14.
70 See http://www.heise.de/newsticker/Frankreich-schlaegt-europaeische-Root-fuer-das-Internet-der-Dinge-vor--/meldung/116995.
71 See http://www.afilias.info/.
72 Afilias White Paper, 2.
73 WEBER, Legal Environment, 525.
74 Afilias White Paper, 5.
75 EPCglobal, Object Naming Service (ONS) Version 1.0.1, para 6.1.

net Service Provider (ISP) would look up the DNS service at the root servers for one "dot" part and get referred to the next DNS service from there. This process is repeated until the answer is a referral to an electronic system such as EPCIS or an EPC Discovery Service which can provide the requested information.[76]

Using such an example of supply chains, Afilias proposes an ONS model with local control and global interoperability, notwithstanding the fact that the IoT will be broader than just supply chain elements thereof. Different DNS operators are employed at each level of DNS resolution. In addition, the traffic volume can be disbursed at the lower, distributed levels of DNS delegation, i.e. the multitude of root servers already existing in the DNS will be used to search for information through an EPC and the ONS.[77]

2.5 Assessment of the Various Approaches

All of the three approaches to a multipolar ONS mentioned above[78] aim at diversifying the control over the IoT and distributing the volume of data. A split-up according to regions is the solution most often asked for by stakeholders and the doctrine. However, the suggestion made by Afilias seems more promising.

While a central root continues to exist at the top level, control is referred to lower instances at a local level. Herewith, global interoperability can be assured, but referrals are still able to administrate the IoT within their own level (of course having to follow the principles set by the central root). Such a distribution of control goes in hand with the disbursement of traffic volume, without impairing global accessibility or an unclear fragmentation of attribution of queries. Furthermore, this system is compatible with the existing DNS and can be built on it.

An additional point in the decision on a particular system is the length of the information path. Short information paths increase the robustness of the system and thereby increase security.[79] A central root with referrals to instances at lower levels do not create excessively long information paths for users and are therefore suitable for the creation of a safe IoT.

---

76 For examples see Afilias White Paper, 5–13.

77 Afilias White Paper, 14–15.

78 See above I.B.2.1–2.4.

79 For the security of the IoT see also below III.

3. Object-Information Distribution Architecture

FABIAN proposes the establishment of an Object-Information Distribution Architecture (OIDA), an alternative to ONS based on Distributed Hash Tables (DHT). OIDA relies on P2P systems, thereby creating a paradigm in which peers have a roughly equal amount of responsibility and data load. Some P2P systems based on DHT are already in existence.[80] As the OIDA does not have a single root like the DNS, this system promises to be more robust to faults and avoid single points of failures.[81]

DHT are a P2P system offering a searching functionality analogous to a hash table, while being distributed and decentralized as well as involving multiple computers without central control.[82] The DHT provides for a searching and storing platform based on correspondence between data items and keys. The determination of nodes responsible for the storing of data is made by underlying distributed DHT algorithms which by organizing keys and nodes in an overlay network are usually independent of the network topology on lower layers.[83]

The OIDA allows interested companies to deploy dedicated nodes, which then form an overlay network using an identifier space specific to the DHT in use. The seemingly random mapping of identifiers to storage nodes more or less evenly balances the data loads, allows for easy replication, is less vulnerable to single points of failure, and reduces the risk of attacks against information providers or users. The DHT provide for the routing to the responsible nodes, and further procedures, without, however, a central entity managing all operations.[84]

In an OIDA, information providers can publish address documents to the DHT for single EPCs or EPC classes, containing the address list of corresponding EPCIS that are searched by users, or even information on the object itself.[85] The document is then stored in the DHT at the nodes responsible for overlay identifiers, by contacting a node acting as interface for users. This node could, for example, be situated in the manufacturer company itself.[86]

The distribution of access to the OIDA and of key management decrypting documents still needs to be clarified. A central registry issuing identifier ranges and verifying the identities for authoritative identities could be easily established.

80 Such as e.g. PlanetLab; see FABIAN, 85.
81 FABIAN, 73.
82 BALAKRISHNAN/KAASHOEK/KARGER/MORRIS/STOICA, 43–48.
83 See FABIAN, 76–77.
84 FABIAN, 78.
85 FABIAN, 80.
86 FABIAN, 81.

However, creating such a central position would render the respective entity very powerful, controlling and possibly denying access of information.[87]

By introducing controlled membership and authorization procedures, insider attacks on availability and integrity of the system become less probable because of individuals' self-interest in the functioning of the system and the detection risk, combined with possible retaliations (legal and/or economic). However, violations of confidentiality are more likely to occur without the violator leaving traces of his identity. Furthermore, external adversaries still need to be considered when looking for solutions to ensure security and privacy.[88] Genuine signatures are also necessary to avoid unsolicited data (i.e. spam) entries in an OIDA. Nevertheless, while the lack of such signatures makes it easy to filter out respective entries, these could still slow down the performance of the entire system. Therefore, the publisher's certificate needs to be verified by the OIDA node used for publishing.[89]

While this OIDA seems to be able to provide for a rather safe and private environment, it also involves a very complex and complicated construction of nodes and layers, which require a lot of coordination and cooperation. Whereas a single point of failure is not very likely, different nodes may now and then encounter difficulties and have to be restructured. As the IoT should become an infrastructure that allows any interested party to participate, a structure such as the OIDA seems to be too challenging to realize and include the whole of society.

4. Other Developments Influencing the Internet of Things

4.1 Service Oriented Architecture

Service Oriented Architecture (SOA) is an infrastructure separating functions into individual units or services, which can consequently become accessible over a network and used to develop business applications. Thereby, a library of business function can be established that is designed to be reused or accessed in order to develop new applications and services. This system allows for faster development times, easier integration and increased functionality than time-consuming software coding.[90]

Furthermore, through SOA, services and devices can communicate with each other, passing on data and co-coordinating activities, which is one of the main

87 FABIAN, 83.
88 FABIAN, 100–101.
89 FABIAN, 106.
90 CASAGRAS, 21.

goals of the IoT. In addition, the SOA allows for hosts to automatically deliver software modules based on requests.[91]

4.2 Collaborative Decision Making (CDM)

The IoT as a framework will include vast amounts of data and information, which will consequently be used by businesses to make decisions. Collaborative Decision Making (CDM) is an architecture providing timely and accurate information that is essential for operational planning, thereby facilitating decision-making functions. Furthermore, CDM allows for predictive analysis in the event of unforeseen circumstances or of disruption in processes by providing special facilities.[92]

Information exchange is essential and significant within CDM. The IoT, also based on the concept of global exchange of information, could exploit CDM as a tool in service and application offerings, particularly concerning improved decision-making and predictability, optimization of resources, improved productivity and reduction in costs.[93]

4.3 Cloud Computing

Cloud computing as a concept provides businesses with computer needs (such as software, data storage etc.) through the Internet. Documents, e-mails and other data will be stored "in the cloud", i.e. online, thereby accessible from any computer or mobile device.[94]

Improvements in infrastructure cloud computing allow for the feasibility for fully running applications over the Internet. In particular, it allows for flexibility of access. Furthermore, cloud computing makes life easier for users because they do not need to install any software, and are cheaper, because many cloud services are free (supported by advertising or few users paying for premium service). For business, the advantages mainly exist in a reduction of complexity and maintenance costs.[95] However, limitations can be seen if there are losses of connectivity or service continuity. Therefore, adequate backup has to be provided. Furthermore, appropriate safeguards have to be taken in order to ensure security.[96]

---

91 CASAGRAS, 21–22.
92 CASAGRAS, 22.
93 CASAGRAS, 22.
94 Battle of the clouds, The Economist, October 17, 2009, 13.
95 Battle of the clouds, The Economist, October 17, 2009, 13.
96 CASAGRAS, 22–23.

Nevertheless, cloud computing has the advantage of lower capital costs, mobility and global capability for access, ease of deployment, flexibility and scalability, as well as reduced infrastructure – these elements are important with regard to SOA and to the preservation of data. However, things in the real world and their deployment in the IoT are not addressed by cloud computing.[97]

5. Assessment

An inclusive model of the IoT is illustrated in the following graph:

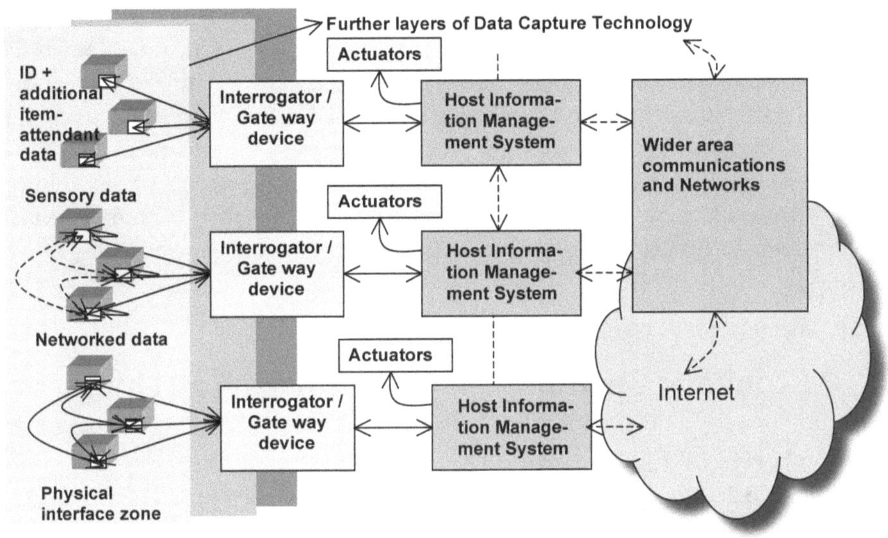

Note: Sensor-RFID structures may be distinguished that
(1) allow communication simply with host readers
(2) between sensor devices (dotted lines)[98]

The dominant approach to the technicity of the IoT seems to be the encoding of RFID tags with unique EPC numbers. These tags are then attached to "physical objects". The information about these objects can be located through either EPCIS or an EPC Discovery Service. The ONS, based on the existing DNS, contains the network address of the services containing the respective data. Technically, an

[97] CASAGRAS, 23.

[98] Graph taken over from a presentation of Prof. ANTHONY FURNESS at the CASAGRAS Conference in London on October 6–7, 2009.

EPC has to be converted into the DNS-format, which can then be used to search for information.

As the ONS is based on the DNS, it inherits its weaknesses and points of criticism. In this context, the question of a single- versus a multi-root architecture is of particular importance. In light of the concerns about the legitimacy of the ICANN[99] as the central authority of control for the Internet, and various dangers of a unipolar ONS, the establishment of a MONS seems to be the only real solution. Various approaches have been proposed, i.e. a replicated MONS, a regional MONS and the introduction of referral systems. While a replicated MONS does not seem ideal, the other two suggestions merit further elaboration. Regional MONS is the solution most widely supported by the doctrine. However, it asks for an additional step in the referral system and therefore complicates the flow of information. Referral systems establish referrals under any existing top level domain and retrieve information by pointing from one DNS system to the next one. Referral systems build on the existing DNS, and are easy to implement in the IoT and be used in practice. Furthermore, they satisfy the requirements of distribution of control and disbursement of data volume. They are therefore the most promising approach to implement a system that has learned from the shortfalls of the existing Internet framework.

C. Economic Environment of the Internet of Things

1. Merits of Free Trade

The notion of free markets implies special emphasis on the economic mechanisms that are to be held free from market interventions through the State.

In 1776, Adam Smith pointed out the importance of free trade for the first time in his *Wealth of Nations*.[100] Smith particularly criticized features of the mercantilism school of thought, such as its protectionist characteristics of trade policy.[101] Based on the assumption that the "intention of commerce is to exchange your own commodities for others which you think will be more convenient to you", which Smith also applied to trading nation States, he found that "all commerce carried

99 Weber, Internet Governance, 106–107.

100 Smith A.; for an overview on Adam Smith's theory see Pribram, 243–261.

101 For an introduction into the mercantilism theory see Thomas Cottier/Matthias Oesch, International Trade Regulation, Law and Policy in the WTO, the European Union and Switzerland, Cases Materials and Comments, Berne/London 2005, 34–37 with further references particularly to Thomas Mun and Jean-Baptiste Colbert.

out between any two countries must be advantageous to both."[102] As a consequence, SMITH argued in favor of liberal trade policies, which were said to enhance the society's public welfare by means of free markets.[103]

Pivotal elements of SMITH's theory were the core characteristics of specialization and division of labor. Welfare was perceived as the result of improved division of labor resulting in enhanced efficiency and thus productivity, which in turn was deemed to increase wages; higher wages were furthermore conceived as increasing welfare, etc. SMITH argued that in a free market, individuals pursuing their self-interests promote the welfare of their community by maximizing not only their individual revenue but also the total revenue of society as a whole, i.e. the sum of total individual revenues. He illustrated this principle with the metaphor of an "invisible hand", which is in the position to ensure the society's interests more naturally and smoothly than any planned allocation, production or provision of goods.[104]

The argument was later taken up and further developed by DAVID RICARDO, who demonstrated the benefits derived from trading through specialization.[105] This concept was the basic model for the principle of comparative advantage, a fundamental law of economics stating that each trading partner should specialize in the production of a certain good for which he possesses the lowest opportunity costs relative to other partners. In return, the State will import goods that it consumes but regarding which it lacks such an advantage. As a result, the specialization is deemed to enhance the citizens' possibility to consume a greater quantity of both goods.[106]

In the 19th century, JOHN STUART MILL[107] even argued that free trade promoted peace. According to Mill, with the emergence of international trade, States do not anymore wish all other countries weak, poor and ill-governed, but see the other countries' wealth and progress in a way that contributes to wealth and progress of their own country. MILL bases this argument on the reasoning that no State has everything, i.e. no State has absolutely no need to borrow from others – a fact that is made apparent through communications among different peoples.[108]

102 SMITH A., 482.
103 SMITH A., 16.
104 SMITH A., 371.
105 RICARDO DAVID, Principles of Political Economy and Taxation, 1817, available at: http://www.econlib.org/library/Ricardo/ricP2a.html#Ch.7,%20On%20Foreign%20Trade.
106 SYKES, 60–61; see also PRIBRAM, 280–318.
107 MILL JOHN STUART, Principles of Political Economy, 1848, available at: http://www.econlib.org/library/Mill/mlPCover.html.
108 *Idem,* Book III, Chapter XVII, para. 5.

Based on the argument that free trade – including all interested partners – promotes peace, a moral obligation could be established to support trading partners that do not dispose of the necessary means to enter global trade. Such a duty could in particular be imposed on businesses. Being participants in global trade qualifies these to promote an activity they are already familiar with and to contribute in a circle they are part of – bearing in mind that businesses also benefit from peaceful environments.

While a further specialization in the production of goods is not anymore possible, the argument that free trade promotes peace could once again be discussed with regard to the IoT. Developing States have not been prohibited to participate in global trade *de jure*, but their possibilities to join the global exchange of goods have *de facto* been limited. Businesses situated in developing countries often do not have the necessary financial and/or logistical means to effectively take part in global trade. The IoT facilitates the inclusion of developing States into the global supply chain, which, in turn, may eliminate certain problems between developing and developed States. However, this inclusion requires for the digital divide to be overcome.[109]

2. Effects of the Internet of Things on Competition

In the economic context, the question of whether the IoT can and will influence global competition needs to be addressed. This issue arises in particular when businesses from developing countries can be included in the global exchange of goods through the IoT.

On the one hand, competition could be stimulated with the inclusion of more participants in trade. It is estimated that the current market size of 5.5 billion USD will move to over 20 billion USD in 2019.[110] Established companies from developed countries may need to reconsider their practices and make a bigger effort and possibly increase their innovative endeavors to stay competitive. Because countries in the East are in the position to produce goods more cheaply, developed countries will shift the emphasis in their production. Different values such as social interactions, democracy in the producing country etc. will emerge. In addition, innovation becomes more important than optimization. Businesses have to seize the unknown and be open, i.e. bond with other partners to increase innovation.[111]

---

109 See below V.A.

110 Oral statement of WEATHERBY DAVID, GS1, at the CASAGRAS conference in London on October 6–7, 2009.

111 MARTINEZ CRISTINA, Project Officer, DG INFSO, at the CASAGRAS Conference in London on October 6–7, 2009; with regard to Switzerland, that means that economic politics

Furthermore, an increase of information for businesses also results in competitive advantages in terms of process optimization: the IoT allows for near real-time measurement, enabling businesses to produce what is needed at exactly the time it is needed.[112]

On the other hand, an increase of globally accessible information about production of goods, prices, and supply chains could also harm competition in an extended sense. If businesses can retrieve information from the IoT regarding production methods and innovations, this could not only infringe intellectual property provisions, but also lead to a decrease in innovations. The incentive for companies to invest in research and development is diminished if any success may be copied by competitors.

If businesses use the information provided through the IoT to harm welfare[113] by e.g. reducing their output, raising prices or degrading the quality of their products, action has to be taken.[114] Free and unrestricted trade is of central importance in the application of competition law, because ultimately, the process of competition is intended to deliver benefits to all market participants.[115] Therefore, an institution should be assigned with the task to take action against offending (groups of) undertakings, in order to protect the interests of the competitors and the consumers. Such action can e.g. encompass the order to reduce prices. Nevertheless, the concept of competition should not be used to control the pricing of products.[116]

Another issue of international trade that should also be pointed out when discussing the IoT is the principle of fair trade. Whereas this issue is not new, it makes sense to accentuate the fact that companies – in the information provided within the IoT – must not give untrue or misleading particulars, use false titles, induce confusion with other products, make degrading comparisons with products from different manufacturers etc.[117] An international body to judge incidents of unfair competition does not yet exist; respective occasions can only be considered by domestic courts under national law.

Considering that competition issues arising from the IoT have a global dimension, the institution overseeing international trade should represent all businesses, not-

have to focus on the production of symbolic goods such as labels that have a high potential (e.g. watches) or highly trusted goods and services (e.g. the banking sector); see SCHMID, Digitalisierte Wirtschaft, 116.

112 See HALLER/KARNOUSKOS/SCHROTH, 15–16.

113 For the notion of consumer welfare see JONES/SUFRIN, 13–14.

114 See also below V.A.

115 WHISH, 19.

116 WHISH, 20.

117 See for example the Swiss Law on Unfair Competition of 19 December 1986 (SR 241).

withstanding their origin. The World Trade Organization (WTO)[118] as a global institution may be the appropriate body to take responsibility of respective actions.[119] While the WTO is not yet a competition authority, its system of dispute settlement[120] could without major difficulties be extended to competition law matters.[121]

The WTO would have to observe trade flows. The organization could launch a complaint on its own if it considers that a member competes unfairly. Furthermore, other States could also deposit complaints. Both initiatives would trigger the WTO's relatively successful dispute resolution mechanism.[122] Claims in that mechanism proceed to a private and confidential determination phase before a joint Dispute Panel, where parties are given the opportunity to submit statements and call witnesses. Furthermore, the Panel can also seek information and advice from outside experts, as well as conduct investigations and interrogations. This procedure results in a report circulated to all Council and Governing Body members and made available to any member State. The dispute resolution mechanism is particularly important when the applicable law needs to be interpreted or even construed.[123] In the event of non-compliance with competition law, parties should then negotiate compensation. If an agreement cannot be found, retaliation against the violating party can be authorized.[124]

The WTO's dispute resolution mechanism provides for steps of investigation and truth finding that could be applied in the IoT. Subsequent to a complaint, an independent panel has to investigate the allegations, taking into account the statements of the parties as well as potentially expert opinions. The report determining the guilt or innocence is then circulated and adopted. This decision can be appealed before the Appellate Body. Compensation, finally, seems an adequate remedy in the IoT, where the main goal of businesses is to generate profit.

---

118 See http://www.wto.org/; for the WTO see also Van den Bossche Peter, The Law and Policy of the World Trade Organization, 2nd edition Cambridge 2008.

119 For the WTO as an international legislator see below II.C.1.2.a.

120 See http://www.wto.org/english/tratop_e/dispu_e/dispu_e.htm; for the WTO dispute settlement mechanism see also Wolfrum Rüdiger/Stoll Peter-Tobias/Kaiser Karen (eds), WTO: Institutions and Dispute Settlement, Leiden 2006.

121 Whish, 491.

122 Ehrenberg, 405.

123 Trachtman, 4–5.

124 Brown, 813.

II. General Approaches for a Legal Framework

A. Introduction

When considering the legal framework of the Internet of Things (IoT), it has to be determined which model of regulation should be applied. Thereby, no regulation, traditional government regulation, international agreements, and self-regulation are possible approaches.

No regulation cannot actually be considered a legal framework: the IoT will be too important not to be regulated; therefore, no regulation at all is not an option. State law, as a second method, is not appropriate for a global system such as the IoT due to its territorial limitations.

Consequently, self-regulation and international agreements are to be considered as tools to govern the IoT. For that reason, these two methods of regulation are discussed in more detail in the following.

B. Self-Regulation

1. Background

Self-regulation refers to rules considered by the "governed" people to be adequate guidelines. The legitimacy of self-regulation is based on the fact that private incentives lead to a need-driven rule-setting process.[125]

Traditionally, self-regulation (self-government)[126] follows the principle of subsidiarity, meaning that governmental intervention should only take place if the participants of a specific community are not able to find suitable solutions (structures, behaviors) themselves. Since, however, public law defines the contours of private law it also affects the role of self-regulatory mechanisms.[127]

In principle, self-regulation is justified if it is more efficient than State law and if compliance with rules of the community is less likely than compliance with self-regulation.[128] Seen from a broader perspective, self-regulation is "law" which is

125 On the notion of self-regulation in more detail see WEBER, Regulatory Models, 79–89; see also WEBER/WEBER, ordre public, 57–59; CAMPBELL, 758–768; BLACK, 32–37.

126 See GIBBONS, 483–484 and 509–510; GREWLICH, Governance, 139–40; WEBER, Selbstregulierung und Selbstorganisation, 211–214.

127 PERRITT, Internet, 892.

128 GIBBONS, 509.

R.H. Weber and R. Weber, *Internet of Things*, DOI 10.1007/978-3-642-11710-7_2,

responsive to changes in the "environment", and which develops and establishes rules independent of the principle of territoriality.[129] The legal doctrine increasingly acknowledges the merits of self-regulation.[130]

2. Self-regulation as Soft Law

The theoretical approaches to the self-regulatory model show a multi-faceted picture:[131] In many cases, self-regulation is not only a concept of a private group, but a concept occurring within a framework that is set by the government (directed self-regulation or audited self-regulation). This approach has gained importance during the last decade: If the government provides for a general framework which can be substantiated by the private sector, often the term "co-regulation" is used. The State legislator does not only set the legal yardsticks or some general pillars of the legal framework, but eventually the government remains involved in the self-regulatory initiatives at least in a monitoring function supervising the progress and the effectiveness of the initiatives in meeting the perceived objectives.

In this context, the legal doctrine has developed the notion of "soft law" for private commitments expressing more than just policy statements, but less than law in its strict sense, also possessing a certain proximity to law and a certain legal relevance.[132] Nevertheless, the term "soft law" does not yet have a clear scope or reliable content. Particularly in respect to the enforceability of rules, law is either in force ("hard law") or not in force ("no law"), meaning that it is difficult to distinguish between various degrees of legal force. Generally, it can only be said that soft law is a social notion close to law and that it usually covers certain forms of expected and acceptable codes of conduct.[133]

3. Self-regulation as a Social Control Model

Self-regulation can also be understood as a social control model. Such a system of control consists of rules of normatively appropriate human behavior. Socially accepted rules are enforced through reputational sanctions. The social control

129 JOHNSON/POST, 1370.

130 See GIBBONS, 509–518; GREWLICH, Governance, 291–296.

131 For further detail see WEBER, Internet Governance, 18–19, with further references.

132 WEBER, Internet Governance, 20; for the notion of „soft law" see also THÜRER, 159–178.

133 WEBER, Internet Governance, 20, with further references.

model uses the social constraints of a cohesive community; sanctions range from truthful negative gossip to excommunication from the community.[134]

While negative communications may hinder users from ordering goods made available from a particular company, excommunication of a business from the IoT seems rather unlikely and would be difficult to realize. "Social sanctions" also require effective communication channels so that perspective users are informed about the behavior of IoT participants. Furthermore, it seems that businesses are less swayed by bad publicity than individuals (end-users) are. It therefore remains to be seen, how effective such negative communications can be if businesses are involved.

Either way, this concept of self-regulation cannot overcome the lack of an enforcement strategy if compliance is not done voluntarily.[135] Consequently, the involvement of the legislator seems to be inevitable.

4. Strengths of Self-regulation

Self-regulation is often used by the participants of a specific community to enhance the image of the market segment and improve marketing possibilities. Furthermore, self-regulation tends to be used as a measure to induce government legislators not to pass any formal laws.[136] These tactical and psychological factors, however, do not mean that self-regulation would have no further advantages. The general benefits of self-regulation include the following:[137]

- Rules created by the participants of a specific community are efficient because they respond to real needs and mirror the technological aspects as they actually occur.
- Meaningful self-regulation provides the opportunity to adapt the legal framework to changing technology in a flexible way.
- Since rules are not imposed by a specific authority in case of self-regulation, chances are good that the rules contain incentives for compliance.
- Self-regulation can usually be implemented at reduced costs (saving effect).
- Effective self-regulation induces the concerned people to be open to a permanent consultation process in respect of the development and implementation of the rules. Their involvement is necessary to ensure that the self-regulatory mechanism accurately reflects real needs.

---

134 WEBER, Regulatory Models, 82, with further references.

135 SCHMID, Radio Frequency Identification, 199; HILDNER, 159.

136 WEBER, Selbstregulierung und Selbstorganisation, 26.

137 See JOHNSON/POST, 1370; GREWLICH, Governance, 324–25.

Apart from a self-regulatory stand-alone scheme, it is also possible that such "private norms" can help to interpret general legislative norms allowing to concretisize their possibly broad scope of application.[138]

5. Weaknesses of Self-regulation

While self-regulation has gained importance during the last years, there are still critics thereof, pointing out that self-regulation only regulates those motivated or principled enough to take part in them as market pressure is not yet strong enough to oblige everyone to adopt the respective rules.

Furthermore, it is argued that self-regulation is only adopted by stakeholders in order to satisfy their own interests and is therefore not effective.[139] However, this argument is not entirely convincing, because companies may also be inclined to adhere to self-regulatory norms in order to increase their user base. Users being aware of the risks in the IoT will likely be influenced in their choice of business partners by the regulations these adhere to. Compliance with such regulations – even if they are non-binding – can therefore be a valuable asset.

The main deficiency of self-regulation, though, is its lack of enforcement mechanisms, i.e. self-regulation is not legally binding. Non-compliance does not necessarily lead to sanctions. Possibly, to the extent a contract has been concluded, the threat of being forced to pay a penalty can be a sanction; furthermore, if market participants are organized in an association, black sheep could be removed as members of the association. Real enforcement, however, is not possible, in contrast to government regulation.[140]

6. Outlook

It is to be expected that the legal framework for the IoT will be established mainly through self-regulation. An intergovernmental approach is not entirely appropriate as users of the IoT are private businesses. Furthermore, it is unlikely that a consensus on the contents of an intergovernmental regulation could be found in the near future.

Even if the manifold merits of self-regulation are to be honored, some pillars of the legal framework need to be set by the legislator, i.e. the main legal sources are to be introduced on an international level.

138 WEBER, Selbstregulierung und Selbstorganisation, 26.
139 FROOMKIN, 1524–1527.
140 WEBER, Regulatory Models, 85.

C. International Legal Framework

Consequently, the following sub-chapter discusses and assesses various approaches to the establishment of an international legal framework. In particular, the questions of who should act as an international legislator and what the legal framework should entail are addressed.

1. Global Legislator

1.1 Newly Established Body as International Legislator

The IoT being a new system itself, the idea of entrusting a body with its legislation and governing that is new, too, is not far-fetched. A new body would have to be in the position to take into account all the characteristics of the IoT. Furthermore, considering the complexity of the IoT, this body should be construed in a way to dispose of the necessary capacities. Up to now, a few theoretical concepts have already been established.

a) "Transgovernmental Networks"

In "A New World Order", SLAUGHTER attempts to offer a solution for the "governance dilemma" by referring to "government networks". These are set out as "relatively loose, cooperative arrangements across borders between and among like agencies that seek to respond to global issues"[141] and that manage to close gaps through coordination among governments from different States, "creating a new sort of power, authority, and legitimacy".[142]

RAUSTIALA assesses the viability of transgovernmental networks and evaluates their relationship to liberal internationalism.[143] The transgovernmental cooperation is exemplified in the fields of securities regulation, competition policy and environmental regulation.[144]

This model presupposes disaggregated States, in other words, it sees governments as a decomposed collection of disparate institutions, each with its own powers, mandates, incentives, motivations, abilities etc. similar to the term "government" which can be understood as the various activities of the courts, the parliaments,

[141] ANDERSON, 1257; see also SLAUGHTER, 14.
[142] ANDERSON, 1257.
[143] RAUSTIALA, 17–19.
[144] RAUSTIALA, 26–51.

the regulatory agencies and the executive itself.[145] This approach is contrary to the perception of unitary States according to traditional international law. In SLAUGHTER's view, national governments cannot effectively address every problem in a networked world and should therefore delegate their responsibilities and "actual sovereign power to a limited number of supranational government officials"[146] which then should engage in intensive interaction and in the elaboration and adoption of codes of best practice and agreements on coordinated solutions to common problems.[147]

Such networks can be very powerful and permit international cooperation without States having to go through formal processes of referring authority from national institutions to a supranational entity.[148] Furthermore, mechanisms can be established that allow for a speedy setting up of networks, whereas the negotiation of international treaties usually takes years.[149]

However, the concept of government networks has not been spared with criticism. Although governments are specifically legitimized through democratic elections, it has been objected that, over time, this proposed new world order could fail to preserve democracy and democratic accountability; last but not least, due to its top-down approach, it could finally lead to a form of liberal internationalism.[150]

A variation of this approach is the establishment of public-private partnerships, through which policymakers delegate certain tasks to other actors and institutions (from the public or private sector) that are in a better position to implement the envisaged goals. Furthermore, many characteristics of public-private partnership structures seem to apt to foster empowerment of developing countries, as they enable to pool know-how and resources from international as well as local participants. Public-private partnerships, implying public financial participation, overview, and control, can also offer an interesting alternative for reducing public budgets without considering the drastic and stark privatization of a sector, an option that is often resented in developing countries.[151] However, this concept, too, has been criticized to lack transparency as well as accountability.[152] In addition, public-private partnerships are often perceived as hidden privatizations, attempts from governments to flee their responsibilities. The concern has also been raised that public-private partnership programs might generate windfall profits for

[145] SLAUGHTER, 12–13.
[146] SLAUGHTER, 263.
[147] SLAUGHTER, 263.
[148] MAYER-SCHÖNBERGER, 649.
[149] MAYER-SCHÖNBERGER, 650.
[150] ANDERSON, 1301–1310; JACOBS, 14–15.
[151] WEBER/MENOUD, Digital Divide, 137.
[152] REINICKE, 132–133.

the private sector, by granting subsidies on investments that the private sector would have undertaken anyhow.[153] This concern is particularly present in the IoT, where the private sector's interest in the structure is distinct.

Notwithstanding a certain vagueness of the mentioned theories, it appears to be sensible that additional efforts are undertaken by interdisciplinary research teams in order to strengthen further fundamental principles of transgovernmental networks.

b) Proposal for a New International Legislator

As mentioned, given the globality of the IoT, the introduction of an international legislator may be required to satisfy the interests of civil society globally.

Translated into terms of the governance of the IoT, this approach leads to a model of a governance body, formed by the networks achieved through negotiations at an international level. Such kind of forum for government officials specialized on IoT issues would permit coordination on a global level and create a new authority responsible and accountable for IoT governance. The focus would have to be set on a limited number of supranational government officials whose networks would take due account of already existing international organizations, corporations, NGOs and other actors in the transnational society.[154]

While the establishment of a new body seems sensible in the context of the IoT which is also a new system, composing such a body of only government officials is not appropriate. The IoT as a framework used by private entities should be governed at least partly by representatives from the private sector. Furthermore, scholars engaged in research of issues of the IoT could equally be in the position to provide valuable inputs. Therefore, a mixture of government officials, representatives of the private sector and scholars seems to be most appropriate to represent a body yet to be established.

However, the creation of such a body presents challenging questions. In particular, an election mechanism needs to be developed that ensures equal participation of all regions, as well as of the three different categories of participants. Such a mechanism is of utmost importance for legitimacy and accountability of the governing body.

National democratic elections can serve to determine government representatives for the governing body. However, the inclusion of all users of the IoT in the election process of representatives from the business sector may not be very practical.

153 WEBER/MENOUD, Digital Divide, 145.
154 SLAUGHTER, 262–263.

An election process established within trade unions which are experienced in the representation of businesses may come to help. This concept still presupposes that all businesses using the IoT are also members of trade unions which may not be the case. As for scholars, such are not (yet) numerous and could be elected by the academic community, taking into account the various aspects of the IoT (e.g. technicity, legal questions etc.).

Finally, the election of a governing body – whatever mechanism is used therefore – will take quite some time. The IoT is not yet in full function and the establishment of a governing body may therefore not seem too urgent. Nevertheless, it is highly probable that such a body will not be functional in time, particularly taking into account that this body should be operating before legal problems related to the IoT occur, because regulations would have to be established by the governing body ahead of an extensive IoT use.

1.2 Existing Body as International Legislator

An alternative to the creation of a new body is to integrate the tasks of an international legislator for the IoT into an existing organization. Bearing in mind the globality of the IoT, this organization must have a certain territorial application. Furthermore, the organization should have a structure that allows for the inclusion of a body only responsible for the IoT. Finally, legislation and rule-making governing of the IoT should be encompassed by the overhead responsibilities of the organization to be appointed.

a) WTO

Following the GATT regime according to the Havana Charter of 1948 which has not introduced a distinct organizational structure, the World Trade Organization (WTO) was established in 1994 in order to deal with the rules of trade between nations at a global or near-global level.[155] Providing for an extensive knowledge of global trade, the WTO may be an appropriate international organization to also encompass a Committee on the governing of the IoT.

Several Committees on various aspects are included in the organization of the WTO.[156] These Committees have specific obligations and are accountable to the General Council. The introduction of a Committee on the IoT could provide an established body with the necessary resources to effectively realize a legal frame-

155 See http://www.wto.org/english/thewto_e/whatis_e/tif_e/fact1_e.htm.

156 Such as a Committee on Trade and Environment, a Committee on Trade and Development, a Committee on Regional Trade Agreements etc.; see http://www.wto.org/english/thewto_e/whatis_e/tif_e/org2_e.htm.

work for the IoT. By appointing specialists as members of such a body, knowledge and experience in IoT matters would be made available at a high regulatory level.

An advantage of the WTO legal framework also consists in the existence of an established dispute resolution mechanism. The appointed Dispute Panels and the available Appellate Body do provide for the necessary expertise and would be well suited to interpret or even construe legal rules in the IoT field.[157]

In the WTO, major decisions are taken by member States, either by their ministers or by their ambassadors or delegates; decisions are normally taken by consensus. Member States themselves have to enforce rules under agreed procedures they negotiated, including the possibility of trade sanctions. However, those sanctions are imposed by member States, and authorized by the membership as a whole.[158]

This approach of introducing rules on the IoT seems appropriate. As the IoT is a global framework, it is important that a large number of States can introduce their ideas and suggestions. The WTO with its 153 members includes a large part of the world's States.

Nevertheless, it has to be kept in mind that this approach does not allow for private organizations or enterprises to contribute to the establishment of a legal framework. Such action could only be achieved if member States establish consultation processes for private actors before they meet for discussions in the WTO.

b) OECD

The Organization for Economic Co-Operation and Development (OECD) may also be an appropriate organization to act as international legislator for the IoT. The OECD is the successor of the Organization for European Economic Co-operation (OEEC) created in 1947. The OECD took over from the OEEC, in 1961, its goals being the sustainable economic growth and employment as well as a rise of the standard of living in member countries while maintaining financial stability. These goals should then contribute to the development of the world economy.[159]

The OECD consists of a Council, Committees and a Secretariat. The OECD Council, made up of representatives of member States and the European Commission, has decision-making powers. The Committees also include representatives of member States and discuss specific areas. The Secretariat is responsible for

---

157 See above I.C.2.

158 See http://www.wto.org/english/thewto_e/whatis_e/tif_e/org1_e.htm.

159 See http://www.oecd.org/pages/0,3417,en_36734052_36761863_1_1_1_1_1,00.html; see also WEBER, Information Society, 39–40.

supporting the activities of the Committees as well as carrying out the work decided upon by the Council.[160]

A special Committee responsible for rule-setting and supervision in the IoT could be established as an answer to the question of an international legislator. This Committee would be made up of representatives of OECD member States, thereby assuring an international approach. The Committee can, after deliberations, issue formal agreements, standards and models, recommendations or guidelines on various issues of the IoT.

The inclusion of a special Committee into the OECD is not a new idea. The Secretariat of the Financial Action Task Force (FATF), created in 1989 for combating money laundering, is housed at the OECD headquarters in Paris.[161]

One of the strengths of the OECD is its peer review process, through which the performance of countries is monitored by other countries at the Committee-level. This mechanism increases the simultaneous, more or less identical implementation as well as application of the IoT. Furthermore, the OECD has extensive contacts with non-member economies, the civil society, parliamentarians and other international organizations and bodies. Thereby, a wide circle of interested persons is able to bring in ideas. Finally, the OECD frequently offers online consultations. Such consultations would be very valuable in the context of the IoT, and would allow for businesses to access the main body of the IoT.

However, the structure of the OECD also carries with it certain disadvantages. Firstly, it has to be kept in mind that only 30 countries[162] are members of the OECD. While these 30 countries include the most wealthy States, the power of decisions nevertheless lies with only a small proportion of the world. Secondly, while non-State actors are able to comment, only representatives of member States can be elected into Committees. It is questionable, whether the governance and supervision of the IoT – a structure used by businesses – should lie with representatives of governments, whose knowledge and interest in the IoT may be smaller.

---

160 See http://www.oecd.org/pages/0,3417,en_36734052_36761791_1_1_1_1_1,00.html.

161 See http://www.fatf-gafi.org/pages/0,2987,en_32250379_32235720_1_1_1_1_1,00.html; for the FATF see also Nobel, § 6 N 31–42.

162 Australia, Austria, Belgium, Canada, Czech Republic, Denmark, Finland, France, Germany, Greece, Hungary, Iceland, Ireland, Italy, Japan, Korea, Luxembourg, Mexico, the Netherlands, New Zealand, Norway, Poland, Portugal, Slovak Republic, Spain, Sweden, Switzerland, Turkey, United Kingdom, United States.

1.3 Outlook

The proposals discussed above take a different approach to the IoT. While the first attempt to determine an international body acting as legislator establishes a new body composed of government representatives, representatives of the business sector and scholars, the second scenario aims at creating a Committee responsible for the governing of the IoT within an already existing international organization (WTO or OECD).

The creation of a new body, on the one hand, poses difficulties in particular regarding the election process of representatives, thereby questioning the legitimacy and accountability of the body, and the time needed to establish a respective organ. Establishing a new Committee within the WTO or OECD, on the other hand, would not require major efforts. However, being a Committee within an existing organization, the leeway in its creation is very limited. In particular, the globality of the approach is questionable, as only representatives of member States would be electable into the Committee. Representatives of other States, as well as of the private sector, would only have the possibility to comment and give their inputs, without any legal standing.

With the creation of a new body, all aspects singular to the IoT could be taken into account. In addition, the body itself as well as its activities may be formed upon the specific requirements of the IoT. Nevertheless, it is highly unlikely that such a body will be established in time. It can be assumed that the insertion of a governing body for the IoT into an existing organization will be chosen, due to smaller organizational and formal requirements therefore.

2. Regional Legislator

The regulation of the IoT could also be approached on a regional level. In particular, regulation by Continent comes to mind. The EU Commission – as the first regional body – has conducted and issued studies with regard to the IoT.

The need to tackle regulatory issues of the IoT governance has been recognized by the EU Commission already in 2006, particularly at the occasion of a workshop entitled "From RFID to the Internet of Things"[163]. Comparatively, the EU efforts in studying the regulatory needs for the IoT are further advanced than the efforts of any other institutional body.[164]

---

163 See ftp://ftp.cordis.europa.eu/pub/ist/docs/ka4/au_conf670306_buckley_en.pdf (final report).

164 This chapter is based on WEBER, Legal Environment, 524/25.

2.1 EU Staff Papers and Replies

(i) As further contribution to the increasing public debate and for reaching mutual understanding about the IoT and its relationship towards the future Internet, the EU Commission published a Staff Working Document[165] on the early challenges regarding the "Internet of Things", dated 29 September 2008. In particular, the following issues have been addressed in this document: development and importance of the IoT, architecture of RFID applications as a first example of the IoT and policy challenges in RFID architectures and specifically regarding the IoT, such as security, privacy, data protection, control of critical global resources, subsidiarity, identity management, naming, interoperability, fostering innovation, spectrum and standardization. Amongst others, policy issues to be discussed in this context include raising awareness among all stakeholders, reducing entry barriers to IoT technologies/services and guaranteeing individuals' fundamental rights regarding privacy, protection of personal data and consumer protection.

Emphasizing its ambition to play a leading role in the development of the IoT, the EU Commission invited all concerned stakeholders to send comments on the issues addressed therein.

(ii) Following the Commission's appeal, 36 responses with further comments and propositions were handed in from individuals, non-governmental organizations, other associations and private companies[166]. Amongst the delivered replies it is noteworthy to point to the following papers:

- *ANEC/BEUC:*

The joint answer of ANEC, the European Association for the Coordination of Consumer Representation in Standardization, and the European Consumer's Organization BEUC to the consultation, dated November 27, 2008, replies from a consumer's point of view. ANEC/BEUC's paper outlines a list of principles being essential to the future development of the IoT including openness, interoperability, neutrality, trust, transparency, protection of privacy and fundamental rights, security, user control, representativeness, respect of European values, liability, accountability, respect of the environment, health/safety and reliability.

ANEC and BEUC support the Commission in highlighting privacy and data protection as the major challenges of the developing IoT. Though, in their opinion self-regulation is not the best way to achieve guidance[167] as the pressure placed on

---

165 Commission Staff Working Document, Future Networks and the Internet – Early Challenges regarding the "Internet of Things".

166 SANTUCCI, 10.

167 In addition, more experience should be gained from the application (Joint ANEC/BEUC answer to the consultation, 4).

industry and other parties to comply is insufficient.[168] ANEC and BEUC criticize the term "Internet of Things" (IoT) as being misleading since the IoT is not only linking things but also natural persons, and request the Commission to additionally address issues like increasing energy consumption, risks related to expansion of electromagnetic fields, potential ethical risks and the "the right to the silence of the chip".[169]

- *Amcham EU:*

In its response, dated November 28, 2009, the American Chamber of Commerce to the European Union (Amcham EU), representing American companies acting in Europe, considers the release of IoT rules as premature. Referring to the Commission's standpoint that the IoT might carry a potential for identification and profiling of individuals, Amcham EU is of the opinion that a discussion on the aspects of privacy and security is highly speculative at this stage,[170] since the IoT is still in his infancy and forecasts towards IoT's development cannot be made.

Amcham EU criticizes the Commission's strong focus on RFID technology conveying the impression that RFID is the dominating technology governing the IoT and thereby limiting the development and potential contribution of IoT enabling technologies others than RFID.[171] Amcham EU also requests the Commission to await further developments of the IoT before laying down rules by taking a technology neutral framework approach.[172]

- *EPCglobal:*

In its response, dated November 28, 2008, EPCglobal criticizes the Commission's conclusions as being an incomplete analysis of the concept of IoT unilaterally based on RFID. Considering the moment to make policy decisions on the future of the IoT as premature, the organization recommends the Commission to carefully assess today's Internet technology and the future technological, economic and societal developments[173] for ascertaining the issues which need guidance. From EPCglobal's point of view the fundamental rights of individuals to privacy and data protection are already well established by the European legislation. Within its response EPCglobal like Amcham EU recommends the Commission to take a technology neutral approach to the IoT.[174] Being of the opinion that services in the IoT will not be regional or national but global, EPCglobal requests the

168 Joint ANEC/BEUC answer to the consultation, 6.
169 Joint ANEC/BEUC answer to the consultation, 5.
170 Amcham EU, Response to "Internet of Things" Public Consultation, 7.
171 Amcham EU, Response to "Internet of Things" Public Consultation, 4.
172 Amcham EU, Response to "Internet of Things" Public Consultation, 4.
173 EPCglobal, Response to the EU Commission Staff Working Document, 2.
174 EPCglobal, Response to the EU Commission Staff Working Document, 2.

Commission to encourage a comprehensive dialogue representing all stakeholders.

- *EuroCommerce:*

EuroCommerce, an association for retail, wholesale and international trade interests, agrees in its position paper, dated November 28, 2008, with the Commission's position regarding self-regulation which (contrary to ANEC/BEUC) is considered to be the best way to properly implement data protection legislation in the whole value chain by leaving users' flexibility for adapting to the rapidly evolving RFID technology and its applications.[175] Appreciating the Commission's Staff Working Document as being a starting point for an important discussion[176] the association criticizes the limited and unilateral analysis of the IoT and highlights the need for a broader analysis of IoT's huge potential. Being of the opinion that the current privacy and data legislation is sufficient,[177] EuroCommerce requests the Commission to explicitly assess the current legal framework before making new policy decisions for the future IoT[178] and invites the Commission to convene an annual Internet of Things summit for evaluating all IoT-developments.

- *Afilias:*

Regardless of the Commission's Staff Working document, Afilias, a large provider of global domain name registry services supporting over 14 million domains across 15 top level domains,[179], published a White Paper on "Finding your Way in the Internet of Things" in September 2008. Afilias therein submits an architectural approach to ONS for creating a decentralized and interoperable IoT root system focusing on five main issues,[180] namely identifier collusions, backward compatibility, unilateral control authority, assurance of practicality, openness to competition in the provision of services and setting of priorities towards trust/security.[181] Using the example of supply chains Afilias proposes an ONS model with local control and global interoperability, notwithstanding the fact, that the IoT will be broader than just supply chain elements thereof.

175 EuroCommerce Position Paper, 3.
176 EuroCommerce Position Paper, 3.
177 EuroCommerce Position Paper, 4.
178 EuroCommerce Position Paper, 3.
179 See http://www.afilias.info/.
180 Afilias White Paper, 2.
181 See above I.B.2.5.

2.2 EU Communications

In its Communication of June 18, 2009 on the "Internet of Things – An action plan for Europe"[182] the EU Commission expresses the opinion that the development of the IoT cannot be left to the private sector and other world regions, as to do so would be tantamount to legislators shirking their duty to develop public policy. In particular, the governance of the IoT should be designed and exercised in a coherent manner with all public policy activities related to Internet governance.[183] Additionally, the EU Commission published further information on the Internet of Things in September 2009 in a Strategic Research Roadmap.

Already on May 12, 2009, the EU Commission issued a Recommendation on the implementation of privacy and data protection principles in applications supported by radio-frequency identification.[184] This recommendation aims at providing guidance on measures to be taken for the deployment of RFID applications to ensure that national legislation implements the EU Directives 95/46/EC, 99/5/EC and 2002/58/EC on data protection. Member States, in collaboration with relevant civil society stakeholders, should develop a framework for privacy and data protection impact assessment, to be submitted for endorsement to the Article 29 Data Protection Working Party.[185] Member States furthermore should identify applications that might raise information security threats, publish an information policy for each of their applicationsand raise awareness among relevant stakeholders. Finally, member States should cooperate with industry, relevant civil society stakeholders and the EU Commission to stimulate and research and development.[186]

3. Substantive International Principles

3.1 General Guidelines

Notwithstanding the difficulties that come with the establishment of an international legal framework, the approach should be subject to further elaboration concerning the contents of such a binding international legal framework.

Contemporary theories addressing international law aspects tend to acknowledge a wide definition of international law, according to which this field is no longer limited merely to relations between States but generally accepts the increasing

182 COM (2009) 278 final.

183 For further details see below II.C.3.2.

184 COM (2009) 3200 final.

185 Para. 4.

186 Paras. 5–17.

role of other international players such as individual human beings, international organizations and juridical entities.[187] Since customary rules can hardly develop in a fast moving field such as the IoT, the main legal source is to be seen in the general principles of law, such as good will, equal treatment, fairness in business activities, legal validity of agreements etc.[188] These general principles can be illustrated as "abstractions from a mass of rules" which have been "so long and so generally accepted as to be no longer directly connected with State practice".[189] To some extent, basic legal principles are considered to be an expression of "natural law"; practically, general legal principles may be so fundamental that they can be found in virtually every legal system.[190]

International legal rules have a coercive or guiding effect on the members of society.[191] However, up to now, binding international agreements only exist between States. Therefore, States would have to ratify the respective multilateral treaty and ensure compliance with its regulations by nationals through additional domestic regulation.

An international legal framework has to state the structure as well as principal guidelines of the IoT. In particular, the governing of the IoT, i.e. the establishment of a governing body and its activities, have to be regulated. This includes provisions on how rules are made as well as are correspondingly interpreted and applied. Furthermore, participatory mechanisms for stakeholders have to be foreseen, as well as other fora for communication. The established procedures should establish equal bargaining powers and fair proceedings, as well as enhanced transparency and review mechanisms which enable the allocation of accountability.[192] In particular, provisions on accountability also require sanctions in case of non-compliance.

In addition, provisions on the use of the IoT as well as on security and privacy[193] are inevitable. As security and privacy are particularly important in the IoT where business transaction confidentiality and fair competition are at stake, technological efforts are not sufficient to ensure the mentioned goals.

International regulations should not undergo major changes over time to allow for stability of the law and for predictability. This requirement asks for the legal framework to be formulated in a way that leaves room for interpretation. How-

[187] WEBER, Internet Governance, 12.
[188] WEBER, Internet Governance, 15.
[189] BROWNLIE, 19.
[190] WEBER, Internet Governance, 15.
[191] WEBER, Regulatory Models, 37.
[192] See also below IV.D.2.
[193] See also below III.

ever, as technology evolves, certain mechanisms may still need to be revisited. Therefore, the framework also has to provide for provisions concerning revisions of parts of the regulations.[194]

The international legal framework must include the main governance principles of the IoT. Specifics, however, should be left for the business sector (being the user) to determine, in order for it to be able to concretize the regulations according to its specific needs. Nevertheless, an international legislator should also be in the position to issue more detailed regulations on various subjects, as the IoT has to be used identically worldwide if it wants to claim global applicability.

3.2 Objectives of EU Legislation

The legislation issued by the EU Commission aims at introducing a regional framework for the IoT before the system becomes functional. The regulation includes guidelines as well as lists areas where further research is necessary.

As far as specific IoT aspects are concerned, the EU Commission raises questions related to the object naming, the assigning authority, the addressing mechanism and information repository, the security, the accountability mechanism and the legal framework. Subsequently, the EU Commission defines 14 lines of actions as follows:

(1) *Governance:* A set of principles underlying the governance of IoT and an architecture with a sufficient level of decentralized management are to be developed.

(2) *Continuous monitoring of the privacy and the protection of personal data questions:* RFID applications are to be operated in compliance with privacy and data protection principles.

(3) *The "silence of the chips":* Individuals should be able to disconnect from their networked environment at any time.

(4) *Identification of emerging risks:* A policy framework enabling IoT to meet the challenges related to trust, acceptance and security needs to be worked out.

(5) *IoT as a vital resource to economy and society:* Aspects such as standardization and protection of critical information infrastructures are to be tackled.

(6) *Standards Mandate:* The EU Commission announces to assess the extent to which existing standards mandates can include further issues related to IoT or launch additional mandates if necessary.

194 See also WEBER, Regulatory Models, 38–39.

(7) *Research and Development:* IoT needs to become a key topic in the ongoing FP7 research projects.

(8) *Public-Private Partnership:* The IoT should become an additional part of the envisaged setting-up of public-private partnerships.

(9) *Innovation and pilot projects:* The EU Commission considers promoting the deployment of IoT applications by launching specific pilot projects.

(10) *Institutional Awareness:* Through increased information flow to European institutions awareness about IoT development should be improved.

(11) *International dialogue:* The EU Commission envisages intensifying the dialogues on all IoT aspects with its international partners.

(12) *RFID in recycling lines:* The EU Commission intends to launch a study assessing the possibility that the presence of tags can have on the recycling of objects.

(13) *Measuring the uptake:* Information on the use of RFID technologies should allow identifying their degree of penetration and the assessment of their impact on the economy and the society.

(14) *Assessment of evolution:* The EU Commission envisages putting a multi-stakeholder mechanism in place at the European level to monitor the IoT evolution and the necessity of implementing further measures.

The priorities within these 14 lines of action are still confidential. However, it has been communicated that the primary focus lies on the governance of the IoT and the silence of the chips. The publication of the Action Plan has not caused major reactions; the implementation of the EU principles by the concerned industry remains to be observed.[195]

[195] The EU Commission has again addressed the issue in a Strategic Research Roadmap on September 15, 2009.

III. Security and Privacy

Security and privacy are of a particular importance in the IoT. Business transactions and interests of enterprises involved have to be kept confidential in order to protect businesses and ensure fair competition. While some considerations can be adopted from the privacy discussion in the Internet, other issues are specific to the IoT differing from the Internet in the concerned stakeholders.[196] Therefore, the notions of security and privacy are discussed in a detailed manner before approaches to ensure security and privacy are addressed.

A. Definitions

1. Notion of Security

Rules on security aim at avoiding threats to the IoT as a system. Such threats can consist in the availability due to attacks on the system or the integrity of information[197] and can go beyond a simple menace to economic safety and endanger national and international security.[198]

With the development of new technologies, new attacking tools are also regularly developed. Therefore, security is and has to remain a topic of discussion[199].

2. Notion of Privacy

The term "privacy"[200] conveys a large number of concepts and ideas.[201] Usually, an individual wants to control access to his/her personal information. Three areas related to privacy can be identified:[202]

- Physical space can be comprehended as a shield against unwanted objects or signals; in this sense, privacy is close to infrastructure security.

---

196 This chapter is based on WEBER, Security and Privacy.

197 An example for the danger to the integrity of information is „cache poisoning", a term encompassing various ways to inject manipulated information into the system.

198 FABIAN/GÜNTHER, Security Challenges, 123.

199 For security in the Internet see WEBER, Internet Governance, 231–233.

200 This chapter is based on WEBER, Intenet Governance, 237–239.

201 WARREN/BRANDEIS, 205 refer to the right "to be let alone". See also HOSEIN, 122–125 and 131–135.

202 KANG, 1202–1211.

R.H. Weber and R. Weber, *Internet of Things*, DOI 10.1007/978-3-642-11710-7_3,

- Decision-making power may be required in relation to the information flow: the objective here is the protection of a person's freedom to make self-defined choices in respect to data dissemination without State interference.
- Information privacy can be understood as an individual's control over processing: in this context, the acquisition, disclosure, and use of personal information are at issue.

Three basic features of privacy should be considered:[203]

- *Secrecy,* i.e. information known about an individual;
- *Anonymity,* i.e. attention paid to an individual;
- *Solitude,* i.e. access to an individual.

Privacy is not a value in itself, but the decisive factor consists in the relation between a person and specific information.[204] The right to privacy can be considered as either a basic and inalienable human right, or as a personal right or possession.[205] Particularly sensitive data vary in relevance depending on the person in question, since information always has a certain value in the information society.[206] Ultimately, the most important objective of privacy is the prevention of improper use of personal information.[207]

Therefore, a number of general principles should be taken into account as milestones of an online privacy system:[208]

- *Choice:* Individuals should have the choice of sharing or not sharing their information.
- *Ease of use:* The technical system should be designed so that the execution of choices by individuals is not too cumbersome in respect to privacy protection.
- *Notification:* Individuals whose information is used by third persons must be notified about such use.
- *Verification:* The legal framework should provide means to verify if the information is correct and if existing privacy policies are followed.
- *Enforcement and redress:* The legal framework should provide mechanisms which ensure compliance with privacy policies and give recourse for legal action.

203 Weber, Internet Governance, 237; see also Benghozi/Bureau/Massit-Folléa, 135–136.
204 Weber, Regulatory Models, 150.
205 Gürses/Berendt/Santhen, 54.
206 Reidenberg, 1323.
207 Kang, 1214–15.
208 Basho, 1510.

Notwithstanding the fact that privacy constitutes a human right, certain counter-values do exist that contradict individual control over personal information. Two aspects are noteworthy:

- Information privacy causes the risk of strict control by the information "owner" and can jeopardize the truthfulness of certain data.[209] Criminal activities might even be hidden; RICHARD POSNER refers to the invasions of privacy as self-defense against deception.[210]
- Information privacy may in the long term, but not necessarily, lead to informational quarantine; therefore the legal framework should be drafted in such a way that an individual can exercise control of data dissemination, however, within reasonable limits.[211]

3. Relation between Security and Privacy

Privacy allows keeping certain information and data confidential.[212] However, efforts to safeguard security might create barriers and roadblocks to others' freedom of action; shielding data from others eventually impinges on their ability to learn and to make decisions which protect their interests.[213] Furthermore, extensive privacy might cause problems in case of criminal behavior of the concerned person and could even lead to an evasion of accountability for harm done to others.

In particular, as far as attacks on the IoT are concerned, the controlling entity or governments need to have access to data and have to be enabled to collect the data necessary for the surveillance in the public interest. Obviously, due process must ensure that the collection of such data does not produce political abuses. Normally, in such situations, an interest balancing test should apply; however, the yardstick of such "trade-offs" is often rather discretionary. Therefore, attempts to bridge the wide discretion and to develop guidelines for an interests balancing test are of importance.[214]

[209] KANG, 1218–19.
[210] See POSNER, 395.
[211] WEBER, Regulatory Models, 152.
[212] This chapter is based on WEBER, Internet Governance, 240.
[213] MUELLER, Internet Freedom, 5.
[214] See BENDRATH/JØRGENSEN, 367.

B. Security and Privacy Needs

1. Threats to Security and Privacy

The technical architecture of the IoT[215] has an impact on the security and privacy of the involved stakeholders. Risks created through a lack of confidentiality in the IoT include economic espionage, and unauthorized disclosure of commodity flows and business relations.[216]

Denial-of-service-attacks[217] are probably the biggest threat to the security of the IoT. Denial-of-service-attacks typically involve the overflow of a network device with more requests than it can process, leading to an overload that renders the service unable to answer legitimate requests. Furthermore, denial-of-service attacks could also be organized by attackers preventing RFID tags from functioning (e.g. by deactivating them).[218] Other security threats include the cloning of RFID tags, the emulation of RFID tags which can then create fake tag responses, or the traditional „hacking“ attacks condensing down malware so that they fit onto an RFID tag. Attacks could then be launched from these tags. RFID malware encompasses RFID exploits, RFID worms, and RFID viruses.[219]

Criminals could also vandalize databases (e.g. EPCIS databases) for the purpose of extortion or to cripple competition. The prevention of fair competition is particularly important in the IoT, since (at least at the beginning) not mainly individuals use the framework (such is the case in the Internet), but businesses.[220]

Spamming, a widely known problem in the Internet, could also affect the IoT. For example, criminals could change EPCs, so that tags point to banner ads instead of an ONS server, which would result in revenue for the spammer for each tag read.[221]

---

215 See above I.B.

216 Deutsches Bundesministerium für Wirtschaft und Technologie, 25.

217 Denial-of-service-attacks are used in the framework of the Internet in particular for financial gains, extorting individuals or companies by threating them of such an attack; JAKOBSSON/RAMZAN, 33 and 315–316.

218 JAKOBSSON/RAMZAN, 93.

219 JAKOBSSON/RAMZAN, 92–93.

220 An example of such an attack can be illustrated with the use of RFID transponders by Ford Motor Company. Ford Motor Company uses these transponders on every vehicle manufactured in the US. When a car enters the painting booth, the RFID transponders inquires from the database the correct paint code and then transmits this information to a robot which selects the paint and spray-paints the car. A vandalized tag could in this scenario cause serious financial damage and/or hurt the public image of the company; JAKOBSSON/RAMZAN, 95.

221 JAKOBSSON/RAMZAN, 96.

Avoiding the tracking of individuals is a privacy need. The attribution of tags to objects may not be known to its user, and there might not be an acoustic or visual signal to draw the attention of the object's user. Thereby, individuals can be followed without them even knowing about it and would leave their data or at least traces thereof in cyberspace.[222] Further aggravating the problem, it is not anymore only the State that is interested in collecting the respective data, but also private actors such as marketing enterprises.[223]

2. Requirements to Ensure Security and Privacy

Since business processes are concerned, a high degree of reliability is needed. In the literature, the following security and privacy requirements are described.[224]

- *Resilience to attacks:* The system has to avoid single points of failure and should adjust itself to node failures.
- *Data authentication:* As a principle, retrieved address and object information must be authenticated.[225]
- *Access control:* Information providers must be able to implement access control on the data provided.[226]
- *User privacy:* Measures need to be taken that only the information provider is able to infer from observing the use of the lookup system related to a specific user; at least, inference should be very hard to conduct.

Moreover, transparency is also needed for non-personally identifiable information retrieved by RFID. An active RFID can for example trace movements of visitors of an event real time without identifying the persons as such who remain anonymous; nevertheless, the question remains whether such information not covered by traditional privacy laws might be collected without any restriction.[227]

The European Commission is aware of the security and privacy issues related to the RFID and the IoT. In its Recommendation of May 12, 2009 on the implemen-

222 See also JUELS, 383; LANGHEINRICH/MATTERN, 139; MATTERN, Ubiquitous Computing, 18–19; for threats of ubiquitous computing in general see CĂS JOHANN, Privacy in Pervasive Computing Environments – A Contradiction in Terms?, IEEE Technology and Science Management, Spring 2005, 24–33, at 26–28.

223 MATTERN, Ubiquitous Computing, 24.

224 FABIAN/GÜNTHER, Distributed ONS, 1225.

225 For authentication in general see JAKOBSSON/RAMZAN, 484–509; for RFID authentication see JUELS, 384–385; WEBER/WILLI, 249.

226 See also GRUMMT/MÜLLER.

227 WEBER/WILLI, 245–253; SCHMID, Radio Frequency Identification, 196; see also FABIAN/GÜNTHER/SPIEKERMANN; MÜLLER/HANDY, 13.

tation of privacy and data protection principles in applications supported by radio-frequency identification,[228] the European Commission invited member States to provide guidance on the design and operation of RFID applications in a lawful, ethical and socially and politically acceptable way, respecting the right to privacy and ensuring protection of personal data (No. 1). In particular, the Recommendation outlines measures to be taken for the deployment of RFID application to see to it that national legislation is complying with the EU Data Protection Directives 95/46, 99/5 and 2002/58 (No. 2). Member States should ensure that industry, in collaboration with relevant civil society stakeholders, develops a framework for privacy and data protection impact assessments (No. 4); this framework should be submitted to the Article 29 Data Protection Working Party within 12 months. Operators are asked to conduct an assessment of the implications of the application implementation for the protection of personal data and privacy and take appropriate technical and organizational measures to ensure the protection of personal data and privacy (No. 5); furthermore, a person within a business needs to be designated for the review of the assessments and the continued appropriateness of the technical and organizational measures. In addition, member States are invited to support the EU Commission in identifying those applications that might raise information security threats with implications for the general public (No. 6). Additional provisions of the Recommendation concern the information and transparency on RFID use, the RFID applications used in the retail trade, the awareness raising actions, research and development as well as follow-up actions (Nos. 7–18).

In its specific Communication to the European Parliament, the Council and the European Economic and Social Committee and the Committee of the Regions on the Internet of Things (an Action Plan for Europe), the EU Commission again points to the importance of security and privacy in the IoT framework.[229] The specific Line of Action 2 encompasses the continuous monitoring of the privacy and the protection of personal data questions and as part of Line of Action 3 the EU Commission is envisaging to launch a debate on the technical and the legal aspects of the "right to silence of the chips" and expresses the idea that individuals should be able to disconnect from their networked environment at any time.

228 COM (2009) 3200 final.
229 COM (2009) 278 final.

C. Privacy Enhancing Technologies (PET)

1. General Aspects

Technological measures are avaiblabe that increase privacy in the application layer. A number of technologies have been developed in order to achieve information privacy goals. Privacy Enhancing Technologies (PET) can be oriented on the subject, the object, the transaction or the system. Subject-oriented PET aim at limiting the ability of other users to discern the identity of a particular business, object-oriented PET endeavor to protect identities through the use of particular technology, transaction-oriented PET have the goal to protect transactional data through e.g. automated systems for destroying such data and system-oriented PET want to create zones of interaction where users are hidden and objects bear no traces of businesses handling them nor records of interaction.[230]

A firth category is being developed by the World Wide Web Consortium (W3C) and is called a Platform for Privacy Preferences (P3P). P3P is supposed to enable individuals to program their browsers to identify which information they are willing and unwilling to disclose to the owners of websites.[231] This server-based filtering tool allows for identification and protection against deviations from the applicable codes of conduct in the privacy field.[232] However, the P3P is not yet operating and its effectiveness remains to be seen.

A Public Key Infrastructure (PKI)-like hierarchical certification system should be put in place for data authentication, in order to fulfill the requirement of user privacy requirements.[233] Public keys are to be distributed to businesses using secure channels separated from the channels of communication. Nevertheless, authentication technologies also have limitations: (1) authenticated users can identify tagged objects owned by other persons if they are located in the same zone as first-mentioned users; (2) unauthenticated users can identify tagged objects on the site with a private reader (even if that reader is not connected to the network); and (3) communication between a RFID tag and a reader can be tapped by a third party because efficient and safe encryption is difficult at the current stage of technology.[234]

In the following, several technological possibilities to increase security and privacy are discussed.

230 SAMUELSON, 1668; for PET see also FROOMKIN, 1528–1553.
231 SAMUELSON, 1668.
232 WEBER, Internet Governance, 245.
233 FABIAN/GÜNTHER, Distributed ONS, 1227–1228.
234 ESCHET, 317–318; see also NIST Guidelines, 5-11–5-12.

2. Specific Technical Measures

2.1 Virtual Private Networks (VPN)

Virtual Private Networks (VPN) are extranets which can be established by closed groups of business partners. VPN are a private version of the EPC-global Network, and are more confidential and integer as only partners have access. However, this solution does not allow for a dynamic global exchange, taking into account the known scalability issues and the administrative efforts and costs associated with VPN. Furthermore, VPN is impractical with regard to third parties beyond the borders of the extranet.[235]

2.2 Transport Layer Security (TLS)

Transport Layer Security (TLS)[236], based on an appropriate global trust structure, could improve confidentiality and integrity of the IoT. However, a new TLS connection would have to be established for each ONS delegation step. These additional layers would negatively affect the search of information through ONS and EPCIS.[237]

2.3 DNS Security Extensions (DNSSEC)

DNS Security Extensions (DNSSEC) have been introduced to encounter security shortcoming of the DNS: public-key cryptography[238] is used to sign sets of resource records (RRs). Using DNSSEC, delivered information can guarantee origin authenticity and data integrity. However, DNSSEC does not address confidentiality issues. DNSSEC has not been widely adopted, very likely due to scalability difficulties of key management, problems in the building of chains of trust between servers of numerous different organization, and controversies in the appointment of control of the root of trust to an entity.[239] DNSSEC could only assure global ONS information authenticity if the entire Internet community adopts it. Otherwise, membership in the EPCglobal Network would be small and the global information exchange greatly impaired.[240]

235 Fabian, 66–67; Fabian/Günther, Security Challenges, 124.
236 Previously called Secure Sockets Layer (SSL).
237 Fabian, 67–68; Fabian/Günther, Security Challenges, 124.
238 For cryptography see Weber, Internet Governance, 246–247.
239 See also Kryptologischer Kampf der Kulturen, Neue Zürcher Zeitung, Nr. 227, October 1, 2009, 62.
240 Fabian, 61–63; Fabian/Günther, Security Challenges, 124–125.

The MONS discussed above[241] decentralizes the ONS root, thereby avoiding unilateral control over it. MONS can be used together with DNSSEC in order to increase availability and integrity of data. However, the approach is not in the position to fulfill confidentiality or anonymity requirements.[242] In practice, each MONS root provider signs the key-signing keys of all EPC managers under its responsibility. EPC Managers can then sign (and periodically change) their own zone-signing keys and the actual zone data. Thereafter, MONS queries are to be answered by returning the actual zone information in combination with the signature, which is verified by the user by retrieving the public key of the respective MONS root. However, this method presupposes a global trust structure and ubiquitous use of DNSSEC, as authentication measures may not cover arbitrary DNS names and resolution steps.[243]

2.4 Onion Routing

The main idea of onion routing is to encrypt and mix Internet traffic from many different sources. With onion routing, data is wrapped into multiple encryption layers, using the public keys of the onion routers on the transmission path. This process would impede matching a particular IP packet to a particular source.

However, onion routing negatively affects ONS and Discovery Services by increasing time of waiting and thereby resulting in performance issues. Furthermore, onion routing could only be used for the anonymization of traffic directed at EPCIS servers – increasing anonymity, but not confidentiality or integrity of data. In addition, the question of anonymity versus a need for identification for EPC access control will need to be addressed.[244]

2.5 Private Information Retrieval (PIR)

Private Information Retrieval (PIR) systems could conceal which user is interested in which information, once the EPCIS have been located. However, in a globally accessible system such as the ONS, problems of scalability and key management, as well as performance issues would arise, which makes these methods impractical.[245]

---

241 See above I.B.2.

242 FABIAN/GÜNTHER, Security Challenges, 125.

243 FABIAN, 63–64.

244 FABIAN, 68–70; FABIAN/GÜNTHER, Security Challenges, 125.

245 FABIAN, 70; FABIAN/GÜNTHER, Security Challenges, 125.

2.6 Peer-to-Peer Systems (P2P)

Peer-to-peer (P2P) systems are systems that allow for the exchange of data between different (equal) participants. While P2P systems in the beginning still relied on a central root, the most advanced forms of P2P systems operate without a centralized server. Data as well as inquiries for information are decentralized, and each peer only has access to his/her own communication data. If communication is encrypted, the system enjoys a high degree of anonymity as communications cannot be intercepted and search of data is carried out indirectly through chains.[246]

P2P systems generally show good scalability and performance in the applications. These P2P systems could be based on Distributed Hash Tables (DHT).

It is very important, however, to establish some form of access control. P2P systems that do not ask for a qualification to join may – being decentralized – be ideal file sharing networks where crimeware can be distributed.[247] Access control must be implemented at the actual EPCIS itself, not on the data stored in the DHT, as there is no encryption offered by any of these two designs.[248] It may reasonably be assumed that encryption of the EPCIS connection and authentication of the user could be implemented without major difficulties, using common Internet and web service security frameworks.[249] In particular, the authentication of the user can be done by issuing shared secrets or applying public-key cryptography.[250]

2.7 Switching off of RFID Tags

It is important that a RFID tag having been attached to an object can – at a later stage – be disabled in order to allow for users to decide whether they want to make use of the tag. RFID tags can either be disabled by putting them in a protective mesh of foil known as a "Faraday Cage" which is impenetrable by radio signals of certain frequencies or by "killing" them, i.e. removing and destroying them.[251]

However, both options have certain disadvantages. While putting tags in a special cage is relatively safe, it requires that every tag from every single product is put in that cage if a user desires so. Chances are that certain tags will be overlooked

246 See MAYRHOFER/PLÖCKINGER, 11–15.

247 Such misuse is frequent in the Internet, an example being the distribution of MP3 music; JAKOBSSON/RAMZAN, 20.

248 FABIAN/GÜNTHER, Distributed ONS, 1225.

249 FABIAN/GÜNTHER, Security Challenges, 123.

250 FABIAN/GÜNTHER, Distributed ONS, 1227.

251 ESCHET, 317–318; see also BENGHOZI/BUREAU/MASSIT-FOLLÉA, 137–138; NIST Guidelines, 5-24–5-25.

and left with the user and that the user could still be traced. Sending a "kill" command to a tag leaves room to the possibility of reactivation or that some identifying information is left on the tag. Furthermore, businesses may be inclined to offer users incentives for not destroying tags or secretly give them tags.[252]

Instead of killing tags, the dissolution of the connection between the tag and the identifiable object could be envisaged. The information on ONS is deleted to protect the privacy of the owner of the tagged object. While the tag can still be read, further information with potential information concerning the respective person, however, are not retrievable.[253]

2.8 Concluding Overview

The mentioned technical measures and their advantages and shortcominggs can be illustrated in a table:

	Measure	Functioning	Advantage	Disadvantage
1	VPN	Extranets	Confidentiality Data integrity	No global exchange
2	TLS	Additional layers	Confidentiality Data integrity	Negative effect on search of information
3	DNSSEC	Public-key cryptography	Authenticity Data integrity	Confidentiality not addressed Scalability issues Only one root Problems in building chains of trust
4	Onion Routing	Multiple encryption layers	Anonymity	Performance issues Confidentiality & integrity not addressed
5	PIR	Conceal identity of users	Anonymity	Scalability issues Performance issues
6	P2P	Decentralized data	Decentralization Anonymity if encryption	Access control has to be introduced
7	Switching off of Tags	Disable or "kill" tags	Protection of privacy	Not all tags "killed"/deactivated Used as incentive by businesses Useful information "killed"/ deactivated

252 ESCHET, 317–319; see also HILDNER, 148; KIM/CHOI/LEE/LEE, 363.
253 MÜLLER/HANDY, 17.

D. Legal Challenges for a Privacy Framework

The implementation of the IoT architecture and the use of RFID pose a number of legal challenges; the basic questions of the agenda can be phrased as follows:[254]

- Is there a need for (international or national) State law or are market regulations of the concerned businesses sufficient?
- If legislation is envisaged: Would existing/traditional legislation be sufficient or is there a need for new laws?
- If new laws are to be released: Which kind of laws are required and what is the time frame for their implementation?

1. Privacy in the Fundamental Rights' System

1.1 Privacy as a Human Right

The right to privacy is enshrined in Art. 12 of the Universal Declaration of Human Rights (UDHR)[255], Art. 17 of the International Covenant on Civil and Political Rights (ICCPR)[256] as well as Art. 8 of the European Convention on Human Rights (ECHR)[257]. Furthermore, with regard to the IoT as a technical framework, the decision of the German Supreme Court of February 27, 2008 constituting an independent fundamental right of confidentiality and integrity related to info-technical systems merits attention.[258]

The right to privacy means the protection of individual privacy free from national and international surveillance. The rapid progress made in the field of information technologies, and in particular, concerning developments such as fingerprinting, network monitoring, bio-awareness systems, electronic data processing, and creating extensive databases, have facilitated not only the collection and storage, but also the processing and interlinking of personal data.[259]

---

254 SCHMID, Radio Frequency Identification, 200.

255 Universal Declaration of Human Rights, December 10, 1948, adopted by the General Assembly Resolution 217 (III), UN Doc. A/810 (1948), UN GOAR, 3rd Sess. Supp. No. 13, available at: http://un.org/Overview/rights/html.

256 International Covenant on Civil and Political Rights, GA Res. 2200 Annex (XXI), UN GAOR, 21st Session, Supp. No. 16, opened for signature December 16, 1966, 999 UNTS 171.

257 European Convention for the Protection of Human Rights and Fundamental Freedoms, November 4, 1950, ETS No. 5, 213 UNTS 221.

258 See Decision 1 BvR 370/07 and 1 BvR 595/07; to this decision see WEBER, Vertraulichkeit und Integrität; STÖGMÜLLER; HOLZNAGEL/SCHUMACHER.

259 Council of Europe Contribution to the 2nd Preparatory Committee for the WSIS, Democracy, Human Rights and the Rule of Law in the Information Society, section 16.

These developments offer considerable advantages in terms of efficiency and productivity, but they also entail potential risks. Modern technology provides – within seconds – access to limitless quantities of personal data and establishes the possibility of creating "personality profiles" through the combination of different data files;[260] this is facilitated by surveillance technology, potentially causing a considerable increase in individual privacy infringements.[261]

In the information society the protection of personal data must be considered a key issue, in particular in view of the right to privacy.[262] Data protection should be an essential guarantee for balancing between privacy (individual freedoms and security requirements) and the need for information exchange.[263] One of the possibilities to protect privacy might be the establishment of counter-surveillance committees, which could mitigate national and private surveillance and help legislate a privacy protection act.[264] To be addressed is, furthermore, the difficulty of how netizens can be protected from the manifold threats to their privacy in the online world, which may come from both the States (for example, under security interests) as well as from private actors, in terms of economic or criminal interests.[265]

The right to privacy includes the right of individuals to control the way in which their data is being used. In particular, individuals have to be able to deactivate their own tags. This new kind of freedom is the so-called "silence of the chips".[266]

1.2 Scope of Human Rights Application

According to the classical understanding of human rights the scope of protection is directed against States and governmental bodies which unduly interfere with fundamental rights of individuals. Consequently, human rights can only be protected from interference by non-State actors by way of exception, namely, if the relation between a State and an individual person can be analogously used to express the relation between private individuals and/or legal persons. Insofar, two

260 Council of Europe Contribution to the 2nd Preparatory Committee for the WSIS, Democracy, Human Rights and the Rule of Law in the Information Society, section 17.

261 See also Benedek, 43–47; Hosein, 138–140.

262 See also below VI.D.2.1.

263 Council of Europe Contribution to the 2nd Preparatory Committee for the WSIS, Democracy, Human Rights and the Rule of Law in the Information Society, section 18; see also Hosein, 122–125.

264 See Diverse Issues of Human Rights in the Information Society, section 1, para. 4, available at: http://www.wsisasia.org/materials/patcha.doc.

265 See also Benedek, 40.

266 Benhamou, Internet Architecture, 8–9.

possibilities exist under the international legal framework: (i) either non-State actors can be directly bound by human rights, which is sometimes known as "direct horizontal effect", or (ii) States can be obliged to protect human rights from violations committed by non-State actors.[267]

(i) In general, multilateral agreements such as treaties encompassing human rights are subject to the interpretation rules of Articles 31–33 of the Vienna Convention on the Law of Treaties.[268] According to Art. 31 of the Vienna Convention, "a treaty shall be interpreted in good faith in accordance with the ordinary meaning given to the terms of the treaty in their context and in the light of its object and purpose". In order to provide for effective human rights protection, treaties need to be interpreted dynamically, taking into account the changing social contexts in which they are applied.

The typical wording of an international convention is generally centered around the formulation "everyone has the right to" a particular freedom without holding anyone accountable. Nevertheless, some human rights provisions explicitly mention not only the State, but also the society or the family.[269] A thorough study of the provisions of the freedom of expression in different human rights treaties allows the conclusion that human rights obligations are not necessarily limited to State actors.[270] The fact that non-State actors may not be made party to international procedures as well as the lack of specific sanctions does not stringently mean that non-State actors do not bear any legal obligations. Non-State actors can still be bound by the material provisions of a human rights treaty, regardless of whether and to which extent they have to fear legal consequences before an international institution.[271]

In fact, rules which stipulate that no provisions may be interpreted to imply that any State, group, or person has a right to engage in any activity or to perform any act aimed at the destruction or limitation of the codified human rights may also be considered as an indication that non-State actors can be bound by them. This as-

267 This subsection takes up the basic arguments discussed in more detail by CHEUNG/WEBER, 418–423.

268 Vienna Convention of May 23, 1969, 1155 UNTS. 331, available at: http://untreaty.un.org/ilc/texts/intruments/english/conventions/1_1_1969.pdf.

269 See CHEUNG/WEBER, 420 with further references. See for example Articles 23 and 24 ICCPR or Articles 17 and 19 of the American Convention on Human Rights (ACHR), November 21, 1969, OAS Treaty Series No. 36, 1144 UNTS 123, 9 ILM 99 (1969).

270 See CHEUNG/WEBER, 421 with further references. See in particular Articles 28 and 29 of the African (Banjul) Charter on Human and Peoples' Rights, June 27, 1981, OAU Doc. CAB/LEG/67/3 rev. 5; 1520 UNTS 217; 21 ILM 58 (1982). These articles even acknowledge duties for individuals to respect and consider their fellow beings and to preserve and strengthen the national community and society.

271 CHEUNG/WEBER, 422.

sumption is further supported by provisions which stipulate that any person whose human rights are violated should have an effective remedy, notwithstanding that the violation was committed by people acting in an official capacity.[272]

Despite arguments in favor of acknowledging direct human rights obligations of non-State actors, the fact that according to the current international human rights regime in place, (still) only States may be addressed as direct violators of human rights, needs to be taken into account. The reconfiguration of the human rights framework and the paradigm shift endorsed by numerous human rights scholars remains subject to controversies.[273]

(ii) A further differentiation concerns the question of whether there is an obligation of States to protect human rights from violations committed by non-State actors. If an international treaty is using the wording that a State has to "secure to everyone within the jurisdiction, the rights and freedoms", or the wording "undertakes to respect and to ensure" to all individuals the rights and freedoms recognized in the concerned document, a respective active obligation of a State must be assumed. In other words, States have to actively secure the protection of human rights in their territories as well as regard their general obligation to refrain from violating human rights provisions.[274] To this extent, the classical "negative" perception of human rights and freedoms is complimented by positive obligations. The State is obliged to balance the legally protected interests. Yet this interpretation does not allow for an expansion of these positive duties to a general statal protection of private individuals from breaches by non-State actors.

Furthermore, the general responsibility of States for their internationally wrongful acts, regulated in the International Law Commission (ILC) Draft Articles on "Responsibility of States for Internationally Wrongful Acts"[275] may be applied. A State can thus be held responsible for the conduct of an "entity which is not an organ of the State (…) but which is empowered by the law of that State to exercise elements of the governmental authority" considered an act of State (Art. 5), or if the entity is "in fact acting on the instructions of, or under the direction or control of, that State in carrying out the conduct" (Art. 8). Provided that the action of a private body can be attributed to a State and constitutes a breach of an international obligation, such as the violation of human rights, the State may be held liable.[276]

---

272 See CHEUNG/WEBER, 422.
273 CHEUNG/WEBER, 437.
274 CHEUNG/WEBER, 423.
275 ILC Draft Articles on the Responsibility of States for Internationally Wrongful Acts, August 3, 2008, U.N.Doc. A/RES/56/83 (2001).
276 CHEUNG/WEBER, 423.

2. Legally Relevant Environment

The establishment and implementation of an appropriate legal framework[277] calls for a systematic approach[278] in relation to the legislative process taking into account the legally relevant environment. Thereby, the following aspects should be considered:[279]

- Facts about RFID using scenarios are to be systematically developed; only under the condition that the facts are sufficiently known, adequate legal provisions can be drafted.
- A systematization of the legal problems potentially occurring can be done by a coordination along four axes, namely globality, verticality, ubiquity and technicity.
- The legal challenges of security and privacy issues related to the IoT and RFID are to be qualitatively classified.

In particular, one question must be addressed: how much privacy will civil society be prepared to surrender in the interest of increased security? Good solutions will view privacy and security not as opposites, but as principles affecting each other.[280]

In light of the manifold factual scenarios, it appears to be hardly possible to come to a homogenous legal framework governing all facets of the IoT and RFID. Moreover, a heterogeneous and differentiated approach will have to be taken into account.

The IoT as a global framework also has to take into account the regional dimensions of the struction and heterogeneity of its users. Furthermore, its technology has to be understandable as well as adaptable to new developments. Finally, the IoT as a platform must be in the position to encompass all objects and services in order to serve as a comprehensive framework.

[277] A general overview in respect of the globalization developments which confront privacy issues is given by BURKERT, nos. 11–25.

[278] See also KLEVE/DEMULDER, 205–206.

[279] SCHMID, Radio Frequency Identification, 201–202.

[280] See KLEVE/DEMULDER, 207.

Topics along four axes – representing the most important challenges to the establishment of regulation – are relevant:[281]

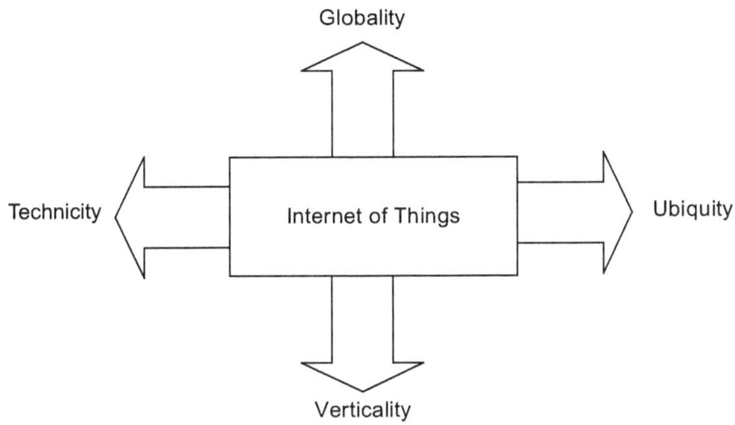

In more detail, these four topics can be described as follows:

- *Globality* is based on the fact that goods and services in the IoT context will be globally marketed and distributed. The RFID technology is also "global" in the sense that the same technical processes are applied all over the world. Consequently, business and trade would be heavily complicated if differing national laws would be in place. If the RFID-tagged products are available on a global level, the legal systems need to be synchronized.
- *Verticality* means the potential durability of the technical environment. In particular, it is important for the life of the IoT that RFID-tagged products are lasting long enough to not only use them in the supply chain until the final user, but also for example in the waste management. For the time being, this requirement is not sufficiently met in the EPC traffic.
- *Ubiquity* refers to the extent of the RFID-tagged environment; technically, RFID could indeed be used ubiquitously encompassing persons, things, plants, and animals.
- *Technicity* is an important basis for the development of rules protecting privacy objectives. Several differentiations can be taken into account, namely (i) the complexity of the tag (active and passive, rewritable, processing and sensor provided products), (ii) the complexity of background devices (reader or other linked media) and the maximum reading range which is particularly designed to cover transparency demands.[282]

281 For more details see SCHMID, Radio Frequency Identification, 204–206.

282 See SCHMID, Radio Frequency Identification, 205–206.

These four requirements have to be taken into account when establishing a legal framework binding all participants of the IoT. Resulting from these four requirements, the framework to be established has to be global, i.e. established by an international legislator, and applicable to every object on earth from its becoming until its destruction. The ubiquity needs to be addressed in particular if various objects are put together to form a new "thing".

This new "thing" can either be attributed with a new tag, or the creation can carry multiple tags. While the first scenario is more practical, that approach may leave businesses with the problem that individual parts cannot be traced back to their origin. A solution could be that the one tag attached to the object makes reference to the different sources of all individual parts. A global consensus needs to be found, which is then generally applied.

The question raised is also connected to the fourth requirement, technicity. If composed objects keep all the tags of integrated parts, tracing all relevant information concerning that object becomes extremely complex and difficult. As this discussion demonstrates, determining an appropriate legal framework raises various technical questions. Therefore, the inclusion of technical experts in the process-making seems inevitable. Furthermore, the discussion also shows that the framework needs to be established at an international level and address all fundamental issues. Otherwise, the IoT becomes impractical and cannot be used efficiently.

Mechanisms such as PET that can be chosen by the users are not central when deciding on a binding law. While PET increase users' information privacy, a legal framework is still necessary to direct industry behavior and achieve adequate privacy protection.[283] Furthermore, PET are, by themselves, unable to ensure security and privacy, as they suffer from certain technical drawbacks.[284]

The following conclusion for a potential legislation can be drawn from the mentioned systematic approaches:[285] A unique strategy will not be suitable to satisfactorily cope with the privacy challenges of the IoT. Inevitably, legislators have to make good use of several of them. In particular, due consideration of technicity seems to be of major importance. Furthermore, data protection and privacy need communication strategies establishing an effective platform for dialogue between State legislators, non-governmental organizations, public interest groups and the international private sector.

283 Eschet, 303.

284 See above III.C.

285 See also Burkert, nos. 21–23.

The establishment of an adequate legal framework for the protection of security and privacy in the IoT is a phenomenon giving rise to the question of the appropriate legal source. Various regulatory models are available in theory: apart from the possibility of no regulation at all, which cannot be considered as a real "solution", the choice is principally between traditional national regulation, international agreements and self-regulation.[286] As mentioned, national regulation has the disadvantage of not meeting the globalization needs of an adequate legal framework in view of the fact that transactions through the IoT are usually of a cross-border nature. Different State laws have even been argued to threaten the technology's development because a multitude of standards create confusion and expenses amongst businesses, which slows down the spread of IoT technology. Furthermore, inconsistent standards complicate the design of the IoT and limite its innovation, because international collaboration may become difficult due to differing underlying regulation.[287]

3. Existing Regulations

So far, the regulatory model in the IoT is based on self-regulation through a variety of business standards, starting from technical guidelines and leading to fair information practices. In particular, the EPC-Guidelines[288] are based on components like "Consumer Notice", "Consumer Education" and "Retention and IT-Security Policy". Consequently, the compliance with the EPC-Guidelines is driven by a self-control strategy.[289] This self-regulatory model follows the well-known principle of subsidiarity, meaning that the participants of a specific community try to find suitable solutions (structures, behaviors) themselves as long as government intervention has not taken place.[290] The legitimacy of self-regulation is based on the fact that private incentives lead to a need-driven rule-setting process. Furthermore, self-regulation is less costly and more flexible than State law.[291] In principle, self-regulation is justified if it is more efficient than State law and if compliance with rules of the community is less likely than compliance with self-regulation.[292]

This existence of self-regulation in the IoT coincides with the experiences made in the field of Internet governance in general. An internationally binding agree-

286 See above II.

287 See HILDNER, 149.

288 See http://www.epcglobalinc.org/public/ppsc_guide.

289 SCHMID, Radio Frequency Identification, 199.

290 WEBER, Internet Governance, 18.

291 ESCHET, 322–323.

292 WEBER, Internet Governance, 18.

ment covering privacy and data protection does not yet exist. Even if international human rights instruments usually embody the essence of privacy, at least to a certain extent, the protection cannot be considered as being sufficient; only "extreme" warranties are legally guaranteed, such as the respect for private life or the avoidance of exposure to arbitrary or unlawful interference.[293]

Therefore, it is widely accepted that co-regulation is needed to secure the implementation of effective principles of privacy in the online world. Possible elements of a self-regulatory scheme may include codes of conduct containing rules for best practices worked out in accordance with substantive date protection principles, the establishment of internal control procedures (compliance rules), the setting-up of hotlines to handle complaints from the public, and transparent data protection policies.[294] Many international instruments, such as the Guidelines of the OECD and Art. 29 of the EC Directive on the Protection of Personal Data (1995)[295], mention self-regulation as an appropriate tool.[296]

Furthermore, the specific problem in view of security and privacy lies in the appreciation that privacy concerns are not identical in the different regions of the world which makes the application of general principles difficult in cross-border business activities. Therefore, a basic legal framework should be introduced by an international legislator; however, the details of the legal rules are to be developed by the private sector.

Nevertheless, security and the protection of privacy are not matters to be addressed exclusively by a legislator. Research and development in the field of information technology should also consider ethical consequences of new inventions.[297]

4. Legal Categories and Scenarios

4.1 Overview

Future legislation encompassing privacy and data protection issues of the IoT and RFID could have five different goals:[298]

- Right-to-know-legislation;
- Prohibition-legislation;

293 Weber, Internet Governance, 239.
294 Weber, Internet Governance, 240.
295 For an evaluation see Poullet.
296 Weber, Regulatory Models, 165–167.
297 Langheinrich/Mattern, 142.
298 Schmid, Radio Frequency Identification, 207.

- IT-security-legislation;
- Utilization-legislation;
- Task-force-legislation.

The different categories of future legislation should be evaluated in the light of the objectives of privacy and personal data protection depending upon the use of RFID which can concern the following aspects, namely:[299]

- Monitoring products (EPC),
- Monitoring animals (real-time authentication and monitoring of animals),
- Monitoring persons (real-time authentication and monitoring of persons),
- Collecting data for profiling purposes (aggregation).

In the context of the IoT, the EPC scenario concerning products is practically the most important application. Theoretically, EPC does not directly trace relational personal data, however, a person carrying an RFID tagged item discloses to the organization using the RFID system certain data or gives at least the opportunity to collect information.

4.2 Specific Implementation

A specific legislative aspect concerns the term "person". The EU Directives as well as many national laws only consider individuals ("natural persons") as objects of privacy laws. In particular, in the context of the IoT, this understanding is too narrow. Legal persons (e.g. corporations) also have privacy interests; as for example in the Swiss legislation, the scope of application of data protection law needs to be extended to legal persons.[300]

(i) The right-to-know-legislation has the purpose of keeping the user informed about the applied RFID scenarios. In other words, the user should know which data are collected and should also have the possibility to deactivate the tags after a purchase. In the United States, several attempts have been taken to realize such kind of legislation.[301]

(ii) The prohibition-legislation introduces provisions which envisage forbidding or at least restricting the use of RFID in certain scenarios.[302] Such an approach is traditional in State legislation if the public community dislikes a certain behavior; enforcement of prohibition is possible (at least in the books). In contrast, self-

299 Schmid, Radio Frequency Identification, 206.

300 Art. 2 para. 1 of the Federal Act of 19 June 1992 on Data Protection, SR 235.1.

301 Schmid, Radio Frequency Identification, 208, with further references.

302 See also Schmid, Radio Frequency Identification, 208.

regulatory mechanisms have in the past preferred the introduction of incentives to the imposition of penalties as means to compel compliance.

(iii) IT-security-legislation encompasses initiatives that demand the establishment of certain IT security standards which should protect that application of RFID from unauthorized reading and rewriting.[303] Provisions of this kind can be introduced by the State legislator, but also by self-regulatory mechanisms; typically, industry standards are developed by the concerned market participants, having therefore the chance to be observed by the respective developers. Technologically, a new "fourth generation" framework of data protection protocols should be developed allowing setting up stringent safeguards as to reporting and frequent audits of the measures.[304]

(iv) Utilization-legislation intends to support the use of RFID in certain scenarios.[305] Insofar, this approach stands contrary to the prohibition-legislation; it envisages making the RFID available in the relevant identification documents. Therefore, the legislative approach has to fine-tune an appropriate balance between prohibited and utilizable approaches.

(v) The task-force-legislation covers legal provisions supporting the technical community to invest into the research of the legal challenges of RFID;[306] the purpose of this approach consists in a better understanding of the relevant problems.

5. Evaluation of the European Legislative Approach

The Recommendation of May 12, 2009, of the European Commission is a framework approach to legislate in the field of Internet security. The Recommendation provides guidance to member States which then have to enact specific rules. While the Recommendation makes reference to EU Data Protection Directives, it does not stipulate any specific provisions itself. The European Commission furthermore introduces a framework privacy impact assessment (PIA), established by the industry and the relevant civil society stakeholders, and the publication of an information policy for applications should also be ensured by member States. Finally, while the European Commission provides for this framework, member States are strongly encouraged to support the Commission in identifying threats to information security.

303 SCHMID, Radio Frequency Identification, 208.

304 See GUNASEKARA.

305 SCHMID, Radio Frequency Identification, 209.

306 SCHMID, Radio Frequency Identification, 209.

Industry and civil society stakeholders are in the process of establishing the requested framework PIA until late 2009. Presumably, RFID application operators will conduct PIAs of their RFID application, the details of the assessment depending on the application-specific implications for privacy and data protection. The framework should serve to define a common structure and content of the PIA reports resulting from the PIAs, and to provide a basis for the development of PIA templates for similar RFID applications. The objectives of the PIA are designed to identify the implications of the application on privacy and data protection, to determine whether the operator has taken appropriate technical and organizational measures to ensure respective protection, to document the measures implemented with respect to the appropriate protection, and to serve as basis for a PIA report that can be submitted to the competent authorities before deployment of the application.

In particular, the following aspects seem to be of importance:

- RFID application description and scope, in particular presence of personal data in the RFID application, data flows, classification identifying the process of personal data;
- RFID application governing practices, such as policies concerning individual access and control, system protection, RFID protection and access to other parties;
- Accountability of operators towards authorities and the public as well as ongoing review of all PIAs, including ongoing reviews and updates of new PIAs;
- Analysis and resolution, such as compliance and legal determination of categories indicating the privacy implications.

The European Commission's Communication of June 18, 2009 on the "Internet of Things – An action plan for Europe"[307] also points to the necessity of establishing a mechanism for continuous monitoring of the IoT with regard to privacy and data protection. In particular, the Communication sees the respective issue as a responsibility of European legislators, and argues that public policy issues should not be left for civil society to regulate.

The regulatory approach of the European Commission consists of vague framework guidelines which address many aspects without considering the merits of the self-regulatory models and industry standardization. The framework is formulated in an open way and thereby ensures that the principles of verticality, ubiquity and technicity can be taken into account. However, being established by the European Commission, it is only applicable for member States in Europe and not glob-

[307] COM (2009) 278 final.

ally. Moreover, the fact that it is up to member States should establish more detailed regulation is even more prejudicial to the principle of globality.

Nevertheless, the recent Recommendation and Communication by the European Commission attest that privacy and data protection problems in the field of the Internet of Things are taken seriously and that there is a strong will to establish mechanisms to ensure that those do not become accurate once the Internet of Things operates large-scale.

E. Responsibility for Violations of Privacy

1. Liability Issues

If violations of privacy occur, the individual might consider to hold someone accountable. First, he/she would like to be compensated for the violation. Second, this liability may also increase attention of the responsible body to make sure that violations do not occur again.

It has to be determined which body within the IoT structure can be held liable should violations of privacy or confidentiality occur. In the Internet, the tendency is to try to hold Internet providers liable,[308] in particular with regard to the dissemination of illegal content on the Internet. In principle, a distinction is possible between Internet providers "providing access to the Internet" and providers offering other services, in particular "providing hosting content".[309] The degree of liability is established according to this distinction.[310] Consequently, those intermediary carriers in the Internet who have no actual knowledge of the content may be held legally liable next to the actual speakers or writers uttering or expressing offensive speech. Their culpability is closely linked to the architectural design of the Internet that enables control to move from end-to-end law enforcement to an intermediate stage of information restriction. As a result, intermediaries are enlisted to block or inspect packets of information.[311]

In the IoT, businesses will upload information concerning their products themselves, there will not be IoT providers offering services such as the provision of hosting content. Nevertheless, providers will have to be established that provide for access to the IoT. However, it does not seem to be justified to hold providers liable for infrictions of privacy by users simply because they are the organ grant-

308 To this issue see CHEUNG/WEBER, 403–477.

309 Council Directive 2000/31/EC, 2000 O.J. L 178, 1–16 (E-Commerce-Directive).

310 See WEBER/WEBER, ordre public, 71.

311 CHEUNG/WEBER, 408–409.

ing access in the first place. It is impossible for providers to establish that individuals they grant access to are not and will not be engaging in illegal activities. Servers are not likely to be able to provide effective, efficient, and economic means of control. Furthermore, servers may have to consider content that has been issued in jurisdictions other than the home jurisdiction of the server; regulations on security and privacy may therefore differ accordingly.

Furthermore, if servers would be held liable for invasions of privacy, an approach to "over-blocking" could emerge, as it has been criticized in the Internet. When Internet Service Providers (ISP) are required to filter objectionable materials, they often have to respond quickly and will adopt the cheapest means to do so, resorting to filtering by IP address. This urgency, coupled with the fear of liability, may lead to over-filtering, in particular because ISP do often not have to give clear reasons for blocking, but may do so on a vague and political basis. This tendency, in turn, may lead to authorities not even knowing what has actually been filtered because of commercial companies having the technical know-how to become the ultimate decision-makers.[312]

Nevertheless, if the complainant can demonstrate that the provider had knowledge, or should have had knowledge had he paid the required attention, liability of the provider may be established. While it cannot be asked of providers to inspect all the information published through their service, providers can be expected to react if they discover infringing information. This possibility of liability, though, gives room to the question of the degree of attention providers should pay to the users they establish access to the IoT for. This assessment will most probably have to be conducted on a case-by-case basis.

Most importantly, the companies themselves violating the right to privacy have to be charged. However, it may be difficult to establish who that violator is. Furthermore, even if such can be proved, questions arise concerning the forum of jurisdiction and the applicable law.

2. Education of Civil Society

Apart from technical efforts and regulatory approaches, educating users on security and privacy issues also merits consideration. Through education, at least some risky behavior of individuals or business using the IoT can be curbed.

Education should not begin with informating users of the IoT of potential threats and how failures or breaches of confidentiality occur, but with explaining the system and mechanisms of the IoT in detail. A comprehensive understanding of the

[312] CHEUNG/WEBER, 409–410.

IoT is a requirement if users are to protect themselves on particular points. A true understanding of security and privacy threats must be evoked, which includes knowledge of „things not to do“ as well as the reasons for the respective rules. Furthermore, education should not only include single threats, but explain the whole patterns standing behind them.

Education has to be carried out in a format that is easy to understand and allows for the illustration of complex processes.[313] It is important not to over-estimate the knowledge of users. Nevertheless, a higher degree of understanding can be expected of users of the IoT than of Internet users, as mostly business will be entering the IoT (at least at the beginning).

There are two aspects that education must be aimed at. First, users have to be taught how to safely interact in the IoT. Second, the educated user should also be able to discover a potential for failure and either respond to the threat or contact the responsible organization – such a mechanism increases availability of the IoT.

Finally, education must be able to adapt to changing technology without having to update the material distributed to the informed user.[314] The most economically sensible and practically implementable approach would be to appoint one or several representatives from each business, who attend courses offered by international IoT bodies and who thereby follow up on the latest developments. These representatives are then responsible to inform all employees of the respective business about new mechanisms to ensure security and privacy which are to be employed by the users of the IoT. Furthermore, these representatives would also be the responsible for answering questions by other employees.

313 An example could be the cartoon format, see Jakobsson/Ramzan, 404 and 408–412.

314 Jakobsson/Ramzan, 400–401.

F. Outlook

The factors that will influence privacy within the IoT can be illustrated in a chart:[315]

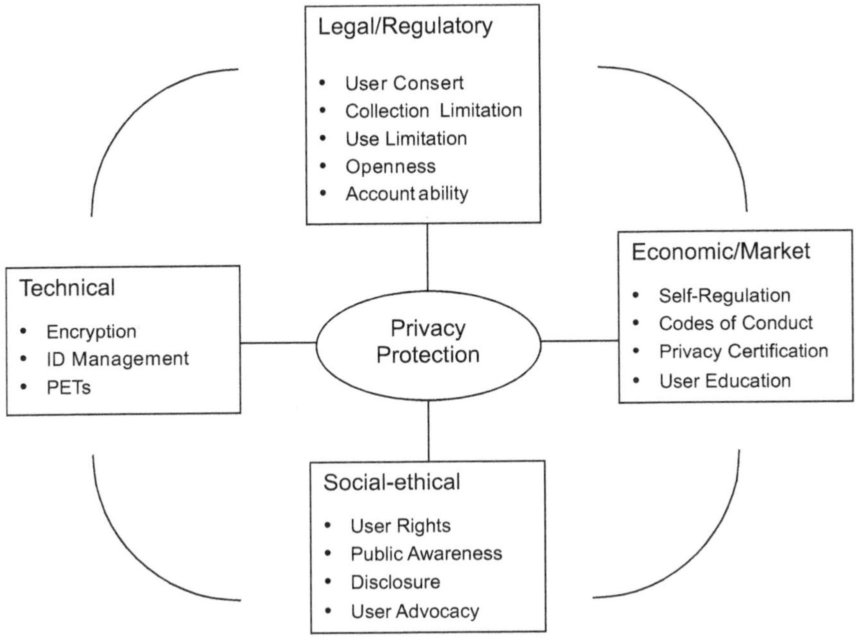

With the emergence of an IoT, new regulatory approaches to ensure its privacy and security become necessary. In particular, attacks have to be intercepted, data authenticated, access controlled and the privacy of users (natural and legal persons) guaranteed. The nature of the IoT asks for a heterogeneous and differentiated legal framework that takes into account the globality, verticality, ubiquity and technicity of the IoT.

Geographically limited national legislation does not seem appropriate in this context. However, self-regulation as it has been applied up to now may not be sufficient to ensure effective privacy and security, either. Therefore, a framework of substantive key principles set by a legislator at the international level, complemented by the private sector with more detailed regulation, seems to be the best solution. Through such a framework, general pillars of regulation are set for

315 Source: BENGHOZI/BUREAU/MASSIT-FOLLÉA, 147.

everyone, which can then be supplemented by the individuals concerned in a way that suits their current needs. Furthermore, the inclusion of an international legislator in the process also ensures the continued involvement of the public sector, contributing at least by monitoring the process.

The approach chosen by the European Commission goes in that direction. However, it would be preferable to have an international (not European) legislator setting the framework; such an approach would better adapt to the needs stemming from the globality of the IoT. Furthermore, if a more detailed regulation should be established by the private sector, lessons can be drawn from Internet governance in general, where the private sector has already marked presence in the rule-setting.[316]

The content of the respective legislation has to cover the right to information, provisions prohibiting or restricting the use of mechanisms of the Internet of Things, rules on IT-security legislation, provisions supporting the use of mechanisms of the Internet of Things and the establishment of a task force doing research on the legal challenges of the IoT.

While according mechanisms still need to be developed, the early recognition of eventual problems and suggestions for their encounter leaves hope that effective regulation can be established before the Internet of Things is in full operation.

316 WEBER, Internet Governance, 17–23.

IV. Governance of the Internet of Things

A. Establishment of a Governing Structure

1. Notion

"Governance" can be traced back to the Greek term "kybernetes", the "steersman", and the Latin word "gubernator" leading to the English notion "governor", therefore addressing aspects of steering or governing behavior.[317]

Different disciplines have addressed governance issues which, in a nutshell, can be summarized as the discussion on the appropriate allocation of duties and responsibilities as well as the proper structuring of the concerned "organs", thereby balancing performance-based strategic management and financial/economic control.[318] Or in other words: "Governance, at whatever level of social organization it may take place, refers to conducting the public's business – to the constellation of authoritative rules, institutions and practices by means of which any collectivity manages its affairs".[319]

Governance plays an important role in the implementation of international network structures. Experiences from the regulation of the Internet make learn the lesson that the concept of "multi-stakeholder in governance" should be perceived as the new way forward in favor of the inclusion of the whole of society.

Being still in its infancy, the IoT's development, particularly regarding its future extent, is hardly predictable. Nevertheless, a preliminary assessment of the current environment regarding the Internet's structure (root system), institutional issues and governance principles is desirable.

As the IoT makes use of the Internet, it is important that proposals for governance are considered in cooperation with relevant bodies involved in parallel developments of the Internet. Within Europe, the European Future Internet Assembly[320] is such an organization. While a global institution would be preferable for the IoT, lessons could be drawn from the works of the European Future Internet Assembly which also aims to develop the tools and approaches harnessing the potential of the IoT.[321]

317 WEBER, Internet Governance, 2.
318 For a sociological point of view see LANGE/SCHIMANK, 19; a political science approach is given by BENZ, 25.
319 RUGGIE, 504.
320 See http://www.future-internet.eu/.
321 CASAGRAS, 73.

R.H. Weber and R. Weber, *Internet of Things*, DOI 10.1007/978-3-642-11710-7_4,

Further research may be needed to determine whether the IoT – being closely related to the Internet – should be governed separately from the Internet or as part of the Internet governance. Given the difference in stakeholders of the two frameworks (global society vs. mainly businesses), and the difference in purpose, separate governing bodies seem to be more suitable taking into account the specific needs of each framework. Nevertheless, close cooperation will be indispensable.

2. Bodies Subject to Governing Principles

Many organizations are directly or indirectly involved in the IoT structuring process. These organizations exercise different functions, thereby focusing particularly on technical, policy, or administrative issues.

2.1 Global Legislator

The global legislator – either as a newly established body or as a Committee of an existing organization[322] – is the highest organ in the IoT governing structure. Its activities concern the most important aspects of the IoT, laying down the fundamental principles of the framework. Because of the impact of its work for every user, the organizational structure within the governing body as well as decisions, preferably including the deliberations and opposing arguments, have to be made public.

The Committee of an existing organization or the newly established legislative body, respectively, has to be transparent and accountable to every user of the IoT. Therefore, information concerning the organization of the Iot, as well as recent decisions and changes should be made available.

2.2 EPCglobal

EPCglobal is a joint venture of GS1 U.S. (formerly Uniform Code Council) and GS1 (formerly EAN International). The organization is subscriber driven by industry leaders and organizations and focuses on establishing a global network. EPCglobal is developing standards for EPC to support the use of RFID in today's networks. According to EPCglobal, the organization's goal is to "increase visibility and efficiency throughout the supply chain and higher quality information flow between companies and their key trading partners".[323]

[322] See above II.C.1.

[323] See http://www.epcglobalinc.org/about/.

As an organization establishing guidelines for EPCs, a key element of the IoT structure, EPCglobal is considered a body involved in the governance of the IoT. Therefore, the requirements of legitimacy, participation of stakeholders, transparency and accountability have to be met.

EPCglobal itself is composed of various stakeholders, and interested parties can apply to join. The organization must be transparent and accountable to its members, being an objective which can be satisfied by distributing the necessary information to the listed stakeholders. Furthermore, EPCglobal should also inform the highest bodies of its activities in order to allow for coordination and cooperation at lower levels, which is indispensable if the IoT wants to present itself as a global information and exchange platform. However, other than to its members, EPCglobal – while providing the everyday user with the most important developments – does not have to publish all of its information on a globally accessible site.

In particular, obligations concerning transparency and accountability have to be introduced in a legal framework. Specific guidelines on how to make information available, as well as on an accountability regime are needed, not only to allow for EPCglobal to know the exact extent of its obligations, but also to provide for a legal basis for sanctions in case of non-compliance. Lessons for transparency and accountability can be drawn from discourses on Internet governance.

2.3 Internet Corporation of Assigned Names and Numbers (ICANN)

The Internet Corporation for Assigned Names and Numbers (ICANN)[324] was created through a Memorandum of Understanding (MoU) between the US Department of Commerce and ICANN in 1998.[325] It is a non-profit public benefit organization with the legal status of a corporation, organized under the California Non-profit Public Benefit Corporation Law for charitable and public purposes. The organization is governed by Californian/US law and domiciled in Marina del Rey, State of California, where its principal office is situated. A further office in Brussels, presences in Africa, Latin America, Europe, and the Middle East, as well as the Pacific Rim, provide for its international outreach.[326]

To this day, vital tasks for the functioning of the Internet are accomplished by ICANN. Its mission is to coordinate the unique technical identifiers' allocation and assignment, the operation and evolution of the DNS root name server system

324 For further details on the ICANN see WEBER, ICANN, 603–619.

325 Memorandum of Understanding between the Department of Commerce and the Internet Corporation for Assigned Names and Numbers (ICANN), available at: http://www.ntia.doc.gov/ntiahome/domainname/icann.htm.

326 ICANN Fact Sheet, available at: http://www.icann.org/en/factsheets/.

as well as the policy developments related to these technical functions.[327] ICANN's aim is the preservation of the operational stability of the Internet, the promotion of competition, the achievement of Board representation of global Internet communities, and the development of policies appropriate to its mission through bottom-up, consensus-based processes.[328]

As the Internet is an important element of the IoT, the ICANN will also play an inevitable part in its governance. With regard to transparency, the organization has to have sufficient power to influence the management of resources in the society, i.e. with a role in governance, to issue publicly reliable information, to define the recipient as an essential component for the perception of both information and transparency and to ensure that this information is available as well as constantly visible.[329] The ICANN has now recognized the importance of accountability, and introduced an independent review of its accountability and transparency principles, as well as the execution of management operating principles for consultation of civil society, enabling its members to participate in responsive procedures.[330] These mechanisms can also be applied to the IoT. In addition to reviewers overseeing the activities of the ICANN, bodies at the highest level must be able to have insight into the activities of the organization. ICANN should regularly report to such bodies on new developments and allow for inspection.

2.4 International Telecommunication Union

The International Telecommunication Union (ITU) is the oldest international organization in the information and communication field. After the Second World War, the ITU became a UN specialized agency.[331] The following years were mainly devoted to meeting the challenges posed by new space communication systems; in particular the allocation of frequencies to the various space services (satellite use of the radio-frequency spectrum and associated orbital slots, including non-geostationary satellites) was tackled.

In 1989, the Plenipotentiary Conference held in Nice recognized the importance of enhancing technical assistance to developing countries, with similar emphasis on the pursuit of ITU's traditional activities of standardization and spectrum management. Aiming to make the organization more flexible, interactive and competitive, the Additional Plenipotentiary Conference held in Geneva in 2002 substantially remodelled the internal structure of the ITU (encompassing three

327 Article I Section 1 ICANN Bylaws.
328 ICANN Fact Sheet, available at: http://www.icann.org/en/factsheets/.
329 WEBER, Internet Governance, 131.
330 WEBER, Internet Governance, 134.
331 On October 15, 1947.

sectors, namely the Radiocommunication Sector, the Standardization Sector, and the Development Sector). This step forward was also based on the results of the Kyoto Plenipotentiary Conference (1994) which established the World Telecommunications Policy Forum (WTPF), an ad hoc meeting encouraging the free exchange of ideas and information on emerging policy issues.[332]

The Minneapolis Plenipotentiary Conference in 1998 enlarged the field of ITU activities to Internet matters, and the 2002 Marrakesh Plenipontentiary Conference addressed the problem of bridging the digital divide and, in particular, formulated objectives to be achieved in order to realize fully interconnected and interoperable networks on a global scale.[333]

With its expertise in the standard-setting for the Internet as well as for the radiocommunication sector, the ITU is in the position to provide valuable input for the rule-setting of the IoT, combining the two aspects. The ITU does not yet have an official role in the IoT, it could therefore only be asked to assist other bodies as consultants. Accordingly, its activities would be monitored by the body engaging the ITU, not by the users of the IoT themselves.

B. Legitimacy and Inclusion of Stakeholders

The currently used Internet model, maintained by the Internet Corporation of Assigned Names and Numbers (ICANN), is hierarchically structured as a single authoritative root with complete interoperability, based on common standards. That the concentration of the *de jure* control over the root name space lies in the hands of a single non-governmental entity is the subject of constant criticism.[334] In the past, major objections have addressed the lack of an adequate democratic and legitimized background which would be required for an entity such as ICANN, that plays the sort of role commonly adopted by public entities. Questions on democratic legitimacy may also arise. Criticis suggest that the views of ICANN do not represent the whole of the Internet community as the views of the community are not adequately accounted for in its organizational structures.[335]

The inclusion of the whole of society challenges the traditional legal and political understanding of legitimacy, and makes it necessary to tackle the general question: who could be a legitimate stakeholder? Consequently, architectural princi-

332 For further details see http://www.itu.int/osg/csd/wtpf.

333 See also McCormick Patricia, Private Sector Influence in the International Telecommunication Union, info, Vol. 9/4, 2007, 70–80, at 74–75.

334 See Fabian, 50.

335 Weber, Internet Governance, 62–63.

ples are to be developed and compiled in an international legal framework; representation only has a legitimizing effect if the outcome reflects the values of the represented stakeholders. In particular, such a comprehension calls for procedures that establish equal bargaining powers and fair proceedings, as well as enhanced transparency and review mechanisms which enable the allocation of accountability.[336]

As already mentioned, the development of the Internet has been mainly driven by the private sector. In view of the fact that the Internet has evolved into a global facility, the IoT's international management should be with the full support by all, i.e. the governments, the private sector, civil society and international organizations[337], and not under the control of one single organization.

An IoT being within a specific public or private authority's power would hence decrease legitimacy and democratic participation. In contrast, the system should be designed in a way that ensures the rules are fair and firmly rooted in a framework of formal requirements about how rules are made, as well as how they are to be correspondingly interpreted and applied. Including all stakeholders concerned with the IoT in one way or the other generally generates a form of reasonable representation, an important aspect when considering the legitimacy of institutions.[338] The stakeholders' co-action, enhanced communication, coordination and cooperation in a kind of forum, frame a central institutional point for the regulation of IoT issues, allowing for participation and dialogue.[339]

The future IoT, consequently, needs a multipolar and decentralized policy institutional setting that will consider the needs of all stakeholders involved, managed by several entities.[340]

Stakeholders of the IoT are businesses and customers. These actors should be able to participate in the governing of the IoT. Businesses must be included in the decision-making processes related to governance issues. Inputs from businesses have to be taken into account and reasons need to be given if the governing bodies diverge from the opinion of the IoT's users. The inclusiveness and quality of governance and the effective participation of more stakeholders would be facilitated by adequate participatory processes.[341] In particular, the establishment of a forum where businesses could exchange their views and give opinions would increase

336 WEBER, Internet Governance, 268.
337 Tunis Agenda for the Information Society, para 29.
338 WEBER, Internet Governance, 102.
339 For participation of the civil society in the Internet see WEBER/WEBER, Civil Society.
340 For more details see FABIAN, 48–61; from a political point of view BENHAMOU, Governance Perspective, 269.
341 For further details see WEBER, Internet Governance, 148–174, with further references.

cooperation, coordination and communication between stakeholders. Furthermore, rules which serve as a benchmark for participation, access to information and transparency in IoT governance, as well as the building of a common understanding of the respective principles and their practice, help the design a democratic environment.[342]

Furthermore, customers must also be included. If customers' wishes cannot be communicated to the governing bodies of the IoT and thereby taken into account, the customers may prefer not to use the IoT but instead refer to other means to exchange goods where their interests are considered.

C. Transparency

Transparency and non-discriminatory access promote the mobilization of civil society and influence the architectural and constitutional principles of a regime, such as flexibility and openness. The achievement of a greater degree of clarity and predictability also fosters the stability of the legal framework.[343] Transparent minimum quality standards enhance the IoT's conditions and the assessment of performance and accountability, as well as facilitate the coordination of governance related regulations. Transparent procedures allow for a certain level of "democratic" legitimization and predictability through active involvement of citizens as well as through certain control over the decision-making processes.[344]

Transparency is not only important to ensure legitimacy, but also to increase security and privacy in the IoT. If it is possible – thanks to transparency – to track back who or which organization has violated security or privacy provisions, the respective individuals or organizations will be increasingly careful to adhere to existing regulations. It is important to inform users not only of data gathered for personally identifiable information, but also for information collected that is not personally identifiable.

1. Principles of Transparency

Transparency has arisen as an issue in various frameworks.[345] Within the IoT, transparency allows for users to be informed of the IoT's functioning as well as

342 WEBER, Internet Governance, 269.

343 For more details see WEBER, Internet Governance, 121–132, with further references.

344 WEBER, Internet Governance, 269.

345 For transparency as an issue in corporate governance see WEBER, Internet Governance, 123.

about consequences of their actions. Transparency includes characteristics such as clarity, accountability, accuracy, accessibility and truthfulness.[346]

Transparency can be differentiated into three main aspects:[347]

- *Procedural transparency* encompasses rules and procedures in the operation of organizations; such rules must be clearly stated, have an unambiguous character, and be publicly disclosed. In addition, they should make processes of governance and lawmaking accessible and comprehensible for the public. An important aspect is the due process principle.
- *Decision-making transparency* is based on the acknowledgement of access to political mechanisms; reasoned explanations for decisions, together with public scrutiny, strengthen the institutional credibility and legitimacy of governmental decisions.
- *Substantive transparency* is directed at the establishment of rules containing the desired substance of revelations, standards and provisions which avoid arbitrary or discriminatory decisions; furthermore, substantive rules can include requirements of rationality and fairness.

Furthermore, various "directions" of transparency can be summarized as follows:[348]

- Transparency *upwards* means that the hierarchical superior/principal is in a position to observe the conduct, behavior, and/or "results" of the hierarchical subordinate/agent, usually in a principal-agent relation.
- Transparency *downwards* means that the "ruled" are in a position to observe the conduct, behavior, and/or "results" of their "rulers"; this relationship figures prominently in democratic theory and practice often under the umbrella of "accountability".
- Transparency *outwards* means that the hierarchical subordinate or agent is in a position to observe what is happening "outside" the organization; this ability is important to monitor the behavior of an organization's peers and/or competitors.
- Transparency *inwards* means that those outside are in a position to observe what is going on inside the organization; the topic insofar addresses the freedom of information.

346 WEBER/GROSZ, Vague Ideas, 131.

347 See WEBER, Transparency, 344.

348 See HEALD, 27–28.

The three aspects of transparency, combined with its four directions, are illustrated in the following graph:

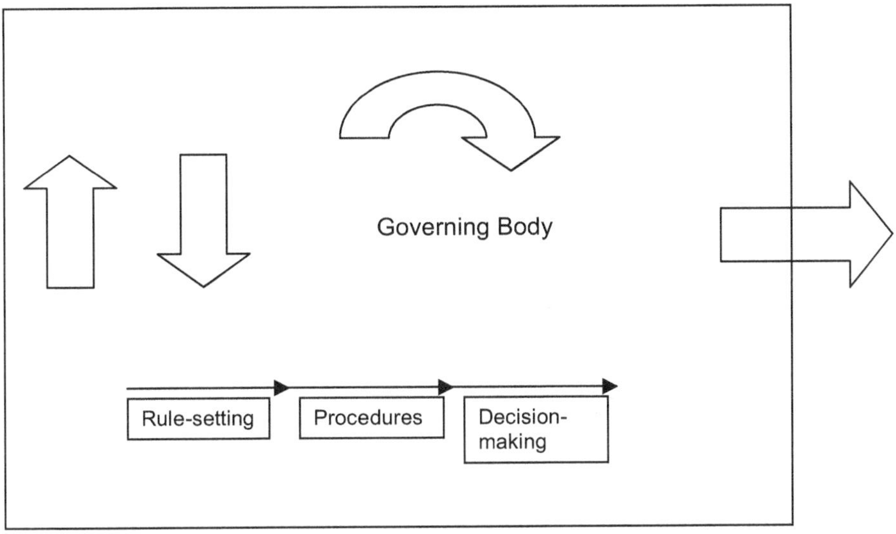

To the extent to which upward and downward transparency co-exist, there is symmetrical vertical transparency. As far as outward and inward transparency exist parallel to one another, there is symmetrical horizontal transparency. Otherwise, transparency (both vertical and horizontal) is either completely absent or asymmetrical.[349]

The current concern for transparent political and economic structures suggests the need to reach a common understanding regarding transparency. This can be achieved by observing the following five elements:[350]

- Availability of an organization or an institution with sufficient power to influence the management of resources, i.e. with a role in governance;
- Existence of publicly reliable information, i.e. substantive quality standards related to information, supported by an adequate legal framework which influences businesses' choices;
- Definition of the recipient as an essential component for the perception of both information and transparency;
- Availability of information, for example by establishing disclosure procedures, reporting requirements, granting the recipient investigative powers or a general right of access to information;

349 Heald, 27 and 29.
350 Lastra/Shams, 171.

- Observance of the time element, i.e. transparency implies constant visibility of information.

2. Transparency as a Fundamental Right

The emerging appreciation of the right to access information can be linked to transparency. It is of importance because it introduces a human right's component known as freedom of information.[351]

Freedom to seek information is enshrined in international conventions, for example in Art. 19 para. 2 ICCPR ("[...] include freedom to seek, receive and impart information and ideas of all kinds, regardless of frontiers, either orally, in writing or in print, in the form of art, or through any other media of his choice") and in Art. 10 para. 1 ECHR ("[...] include freedom to hold opinions and to receive and impart information and ideas without interference by public authority and regardless of frontiers").

Freedom of information is a right of the public to be informed. This information has to be provided within reasonable and clearly defined time limits. However, this right has to be defined by law in order to constitute such a right, as it imposes obligations on others. Furthermore, it is subject to certain exceptions (e.g. for safety or privacy issues) – as is the principle of transparency.[352]

Transparency has also been acknowledged to be a crucial issue when addressing the effectiveness of international regimes. The promotion of transparency is often enough one of the most important functions, for instance when referring to the submission of reports to the Human Rights Committee according to Art. 40 ICCPR. However, the methods with which a regime can actually promote transparency have remained rather unexplored so far. Generally speaking, transparency enhancement depends on the purposes for which information is sought, on the capacity and incentives of actors to provide that information, and on the strategies adopted to encourage transparency.[353]

3. Transparency in the IoT

To establish transparent mechanisms for the IoT, lessons can be drawn from the Internet.[354] ICANN's election-processes and decision-making procedures have

351 Birkinshaw, 204 and 216.

352 Birkinshaw, 188.

353 See Mitchell, 109–110.

354 For transparency in other markets see Weber, Internet Governance, 124–127.

been criticized. Thereupon, ICANN has started to take steps to improve transparency in its governance of the Internet.[355] It has been recognized that generally, a consensus-driven and bottom-up approach leads to broader transparency and additionally makes private entities accountable to the public, also giving non-State actors a voice in the rulemaking process.[356] This is particularly important in the IoT, where mainly private actors are users and where it is therefore very possible that private entities will be responsible for its governance.

Furthermore, transparency must be established for procedures, decision-making and elaboration of regulation. Stakeholders have to be in the position to follow-up on all important actions in the governance of the IoT. Transparency has, in addition, to exist in the governing body of the IoT, as well as outside of the respective organization. Finally, hierarchical transparency needs to be established – superior/principal bodies should have insight into actions of their subordinates and vice versa.

The medium of the Internet on which the IoT is based offers valuable opportunities for transparent communication. In fact, in order to achieve transparency in the regulatory process, the Internet could be used to achieve open access to negotiations, to collect proposals and statements from the various stakeholders concerned, to present the decisions and results, and thereby enhance and facilitate communication and dialogue between IoT institutions and the interested parties. As the ONS relies on the DNS, access to the Internet is a prerequisite to make use of the IoT. Access to the Internet can therefore be presumed.

Mechanisms ensuring transparency also have to be adaptable to technological change in order for them to be usable in evolving systems. With the evolvement of the IoT, information channels as well as participation mechanisms have to remain accessible for business.

A certain consistency of the respective methods is also desirable with regard to the convenience for users. Users should not be forced to switch from one point of access or participatory mechanism, respectively, to another any time the technology evolves. This approach would render effective participation very difficult, in particular because users may not have the necessary capacities to follow up on technological developments in the IoT, except for major major changes with considerable impact.

355 See WEBER, Internet Governance, 127–129.

356 WEBER, Internet Governance, 127.

D. Accountability

Accountability of governing bodies is of enormous importance in the IoT. As business transactions and the information of users are carried out through that system, it is essential for businesses to know how the respective actions will be carried out. Furthermore, if business transactions fail because of faults in the system (potentially involving large amounts of money), businesses need to know whom to hold responsible.

1. Notion of Accountability

"Accountability" stems from the Latin word *accomptare* (to account), a prefixed form of *computare* (to calculate), used in the money lending system developed in Ancient Greece and Rome. Accountability is the acknowledgement and assumption of responsibility for actions, products, decisions, and policies within the scope of the designated role.[357] Various types of accountability can be distinguished, namely moral, administrative, political, managerial, market, legal/judicial, constituency-related and professional accountability.[358] The key elements are political accountability binding the government, civil servants and politicians, administrative accountability addressed to civil servants and governmental commissions, market accountability requesting the services providers to act in a "user-driven" way and constituency relations making the public agency accountable for voices expressed outside the established channels.

In the meantime, accountability has become an important topic in the discussion about the legitimacy of international institutions. Due to the lack of a "global democracy" to which organizations must abide, global administrative bodies are confronted with requests to overcome accountability gaps. Even non-government agencies are beginning to prepare and sign "accountability charters".[359]

Accountability is a pervasive concept, encompassing political, legal, philosophical and other aspects; each context casts a different shade on the meaning of accountability. Nevertheless, a general definition incorporating basic elements remains recognizable in the sense that accountability consists in the obligation of a person (the accountable) to another (the accountee), according to which the former must give account of, explain and justify his actions or decisions against criteria of the same kind, as well as take responsibility for any fault or damage.[360]

357 For further detail see Weber, Internet Governance, 133.

358 See Dwivedi/Jabbra, 5–8.

359 See for example HAPI (Human Accountability Partnership International).

360 Lastra/Shams, 167; Malcolm, 262.

- Standards need to be introduced which hold governing bodies accountable, at least on the organizational level; such standards help to improve accountability.
- Information should be made more easily available to accountability-holders, enabling them to apply the standards in question to the performance of those who are held to account; in order to make information flow rather active than passive (seen from a recipient's point of view) consultation procedures are to be established.
- Accountability-holders must be able to impose some sort of sanction, thus, attaching costs to the failure to meet the standards; such kind of "sanctioning" is only possible if adequate participation schemes are realized through direct voting channels and indirect representation schemes.[361]

2. Accountability and Markets

The IoT as a system is in principle market-oriented. Therefore, economic mechanisms have to be taken into account when considering accountability within the IoT.

In particular, accountability of IoT governing bodies is not only important for the public to oversee the organizations' activities, but also serves the self-interest of the respective entities. A clear definition of the authority of each governing body and a justification for actions taken contributes to their respective effectiveness and credibility.

Contrary to traditional political accountability, market-oriented accountability is based on informal economic mechanisms rather than on highly formal hierarchical control types. A private enterprise principally focuses on its role with regard to the aspect of demand; its ability to attract and maintain users is a central indicator of its accountability to the public in the market place, i.e. the main accountability mechanism is reflected in the responsiveness to the user needs; insofar, choices of the concerned market players are the key constituents for the enterprises.[362] Applying this concept to the IoT would imply that the governing bodies of the IoT would assume the role of private enterprises, and the businesses using the IoT the role of the users, i.e. the demand side. IoT governing bodies should then focus on the wishes and desires of businesses if they want the IoT to continue being an important framework for the actual communication needs, inter alia by being responsive to businesses due to the fact that primarily their choices influ-

361 WEBER, Internet Governance, 147.

362 DE VEY MESTDAGH/RIJGERSBERG, 32.

ence the smooth functioning of the IoT. However, while economic mechanisms can improve accountability, a legal framework with provisions on information and supervision is nevertheless indispensable.

3. Accountability Elements

3.1 Organizational Level Aspects

As far as the "organization" of the IoT is concerned, accountability problems can arise at different levels. In terms of a democratic governance understanding, the most important elements of the decision-making processes should lie in the hands of the "body" establishing a constitutional level or international agreements, respectively. In the IoT world, a certain democratic deficit cannot be avoided.[363] Business only has a restricted influence on the highest bodies of the IoT's "organization" and possibilities for direct influence of the business sector on the rule-making processes still need to be introduced.

Accountability is further affected by a potential lack of transparency with respect to deliberations of the decision making bodies in IoT governance. Obviously, secrecy provisions for statements made by individuals in established bodies of an organization play a certain role. Such secrecy clauses, however, should not be used as pretext for not revealing how decisions were made, i.e. on what grounds and with which objectives. Transparency in this sense is an important part of overall accountability.[364]

In democratic States, governments typically bolster public accountability through measures of institutional checks and balances in which certain branches or agencies of the government are empowered to oversee and sanction others. No such "horizontal" mechanism exists in relation to IoT governance. In particular, review bodies are not (yet) available and traditional control does not exist in respect to "governmental" decisions by the highest bodies of the IoT.[365] Furthermore, a judicial review is unlikely to be installed in a framework such as the IoT which is mainly used by the private sector and whose governance rules do not fall under courts' judicial competences.[366]

Finally, strict structures need to be established on the staff level. Besides technical knowledge, staff has to be directed towards cooperation with citizen groups.[367]

---

363 See WEBER/GROSZ, Vague Ideas, 133–134, with further references.

364 See above IV.C.

365 EBRAHIM/HERZ, 16, related to the World Bank Group.

366 Generally to this problem see PAGE, 144–145.

367 EBRAHIM/HERZ, 5–8 (generally to international financial institutions).

3.2 Project Level Aspects

The technological changes and business needs in the use of the IoT require substantial project work to be performed by its governing bodies. It would be possible to design specific information disclosure or other safeguard policies, which could contribute to the information of the public on such developments and thereby increase accountability.[368]

Furthermore, businesses should have a direct influence on technical expertise. As a result, cooperation between the institutionalized "technical" bodies and businesses needs to be encouraged and seen as a reasonable option.[369]

3.3 Policy Level Aspects

The policies chosen by the competent bodies of the IoT have a major input on the future of infrastructural networks. Therefore, such policies should be checked in view of the needs and wishes of the users. Practically, this objective could be achieved through feedback mechanisms designed to play an important role, also regarding accountability. Policy processes should be consultative in the sense that users are invited to comment on policy proposals.[370] In substance, mainly the respective processes need to be improved accordingly, not necessarily the outcomes.[371]

One possible way to observe the feedback approach could consist in the distribution of iterative drafts of policy provisions prior to their release for comments stemming from users. Another mechanism could consist in the publication of a matrix which compiles all comments and explains how each input was addressed within the policy review, or why it was not approved of. Thereby, users would become aware of its input's potential effect on the reasoning of the competent bodies in accepting or rejecting comments. Such an approach would establish a high level of accountability.

4. Accountability in the IoT

Accountability is regularly called for to improve the governance regimes of organizations. Even if multi-stakeholderism leads the diverse constitutions of the accountees and therefore accountability mechanisms should reflect the different

368 EBRAHIM/HERZ, 9–10 and 18–27.
369 See also WEBER/WEBER, Civil Society, 9.
370 EBRAHIM/HERZ, 11.
371 See also GOODHART, 162–163.

particularities in the various segments of civil society, accountability in the IoT governance would improve if standards are harmonized in a way which makes governing bodies accountable, at least at the organizational level.[372] Consequently, accountability asks for a legal framework providing for regulations about the conduct of governing bodies as well as upon which actions can be measured.

In particular the establishment of standards in terms of specific values that lay the foundation of accountability could provide for a viable way forward. Similarly to a Magna Charta or a constitutional approach, such standards could help implement a legitimizing structure and a guideline for governance of the IoT in general. Furthermore, they would be suitable to entail significant self-constraints for the policy-making institutions, and hence, move towards substantiating the realistic implementation of accountability.[373] Nevertheless, the strengthening of the legal framework by a treaty-related model of governance, encompassing some kind of international supervision, would have supplemental merits since pressure on privately introduced structures has the tendency to improve compliance by the "market players". Consequently, private initiatives are to be complemented by functional surveillance, for example under the organization that also acts as international legislator which can benefit from an extensive knowledge of the IoT itself as well as of its regulations.

However, the exact embodiment of the respective surveillance must not be decided upon by governments or scholars single-handedly. Businesses should be asked to feedback in response to proposed mechanisms and be able to comment policy proposals. Such inputs may increase the practicability and efficiency of the body to be established.

Accountability-holders must also be able to impose some sort of sanction in cases of non-compliance with accountability criteria. Standards could help implement legitimizing structures and serve as a guideline for governance principles.[374]

Businesses as users of the IoT are, in most countries, subject to regular (independent) reviews. Lessons are to be drawn from the respective experiences. For example, an external monitoring mechanism could be established similar to auditing agencies in Swiss banking law. Review bodies have to be independent from the company management (in fact as well as in appearance) and report directly to the administrative board or an external auditing agency.[375] Furthermore, review bodies have an unlimited right to disclosure of information.[376] External monitors are

372 For more details see WEBER, Internet Governance, 132–148, with further references.

373 See also WEBER/GROSZ, Vague Ideas, 128.

374 WEBER, Internet Governance, 269.

375 Art. 20 para. 3 of the Federal Act of November 8, 1934 on Banks and Thrift Institutions.

376 Art. 19 para. 2 of the Federal Act of November 8, 1934 on Banks and Thrift Institutions.

considered to be more independent than internal monitors and therefore more likely to criticize the governing body or mechanisms within the framework. Such a mechanism of supervision asks for the involvement a private organization (to be established), which seems to be more appropriate than the involvement of an intergovernmental supervision, because stakeholders are mainly private businesses and a private organization may be in a better position to judge the needs and desires of private users.

5. Increase of Accountability

Accountability of governing bodies can be increased through various mechanisms, which are discussed briefly in the following.

5.1 Consultation and Inclusion of Users

In democratic States, governments typically bolster public accountability through institutional checks and balances based on transparent information; supervisory authorities have the capacity to oversee certain activities which have been undertaken by lower-ranked bodies and may sanction misleading activities.[377]

In the IoT, an entity with the power to oversee the activities of other bodies should also be established. In order to avoid movements in undesirable directions, new developments need to be examined in advance and consultation processes should be put into effect to help streamline the establishment and the implementation of policies. Consultation with users allows addressing potential disputes at an early stage and looking for solutions within due time.[378]

The design of consultation processes depends on the matters involved and on the availability of active users' groups. However, users should not only be consulted in the preparational phase of projects, but also be informed after the project's launch. Feedback mechanisms concerning reviewing processes need to be consistently utilized – an aspect which would also allow the participants in the process to understand how their insights and expertise have influenced the policy outcomes.[379] Final decisions of the governing bodies, together with the considerations that led to them, are to be published. Only in a corresponding framework can users exercise a certain control over the decision-making process. Indeed, by

377 In general see GRANT/KEOHANE, 29–33; SINGH, 298–301.

378 EBRAHIM/HERZ, 23.

379 See EBRAHIM/HERZ, 25–26; SAUL, 134.

presenting the results of negotiations, communications and dialogues to users, accountability would be enhanced and facilitated.[380]

Accountability should also extend to the monitoring stages of a project's realization and empower the development of effectiveness through user participation. Different kinds of capacities need to be made available in order to meaningfully improve participation during a decision-making process, namely (i) the ability to understand and criticize technical issues, (ii) sufficient knowledge on the given structures and potentials, and (iii) the skills necessary to negotiate with more powerful actors.[381] Therefore, respective assistance to users – in particular the responsible entities within companies – has to be provided by the competent body. This objective might be achieved by an internationally active organization establishing contact points that interested people would be able to access. However, an international organization most likely would publish information only in a few languages, as extensive translations would be too excessive to afford. As a consequence, the exclusion of certain groups could probably not be avoided. If the participatory process is considered to be insufficient or if concerns and comments by the public have not been adequately addressed by the competent bodies, users should also be able to get redress. A means for redress could help facilitate the implementation of projects at a later stage.[382]

5.2 Intergovernmental Supervision

Another possible way to increase the accountability of the Internet governing bodies and to tackle the apparent legitimacy problem consists in the introduction of some kind of intergovernmental supervision (treaty-related model of governance). Intergovernmental supervision is an administrative process in which the central government monitors the processes in subordinate bodies and intervenes to in case of mistakes, based on a statutory authority to do so.[383] Thereby, IoT governing bodies would become accountable to the international community.

Intergovernmental supervision has to be distinguished from democratic supervision processes, which were originally designed to avoid governmental power abuse by letting the public participate in policy matters. However, intergovernmental supervision does not encompass individuals and private entities, but rather consists of State officials speaking on behalf of international organizations, which, regularly, are not elected by the community, but by the concerned government.

380 Weber/Weber, Civil Society, 15.

381 Ebrahim/Herz, 26.

382 Ebrahim/Herz, 27, refer to "social accountability".

383 See http://dissertations.ub.rug.nl/FILES/faculties/jur/1990/j.de.ridder/DeRidder.PDF.

Looking at this fact, such international supervision would not enhance participation of users in the governance of the IoT.[384]

E. Allocation of Critical Resources

1. Meeting Infrastructure Requirements

The characteristics of the infrastructure of the IoT comprise four particular elements:

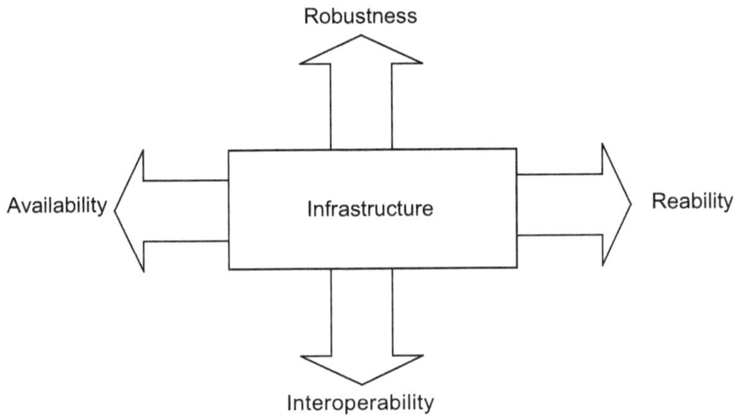

In the following, these four characteristics are discussed under the angle of governance principles in more detail.

1.1 Robustness

A "robust" system is capable of dealing with changes in its operation without suffering from major damage or loss of functionality. Furthermore, robustness implies that the system can absorb attacks without it failing. In particular in the IoT with sensors at its basis, devices should have some knowledge about their own functionality and be able to "call for help" in case of failure.[385] Ideally, the IoT itself should include self-managing, self-monitoring, self-diagnosing and self-repairing structures in order to ensure the permanent functioning of the system.[386]

---

384 De Vey Mestdagh/Rijgersberg, 29.
385 Kennedy, 7.
386 CASAGRAS, 7.

The provision of a robust system for the IoT is primarily a task for technicians and engineers. They carry the responsibility to develop a system that can absorb attacks. In particular, it is important not to overload the functionality in objects. Rather than loading each device with copies of the same functionality, the possibility to seek additional information from a dedicated device or sensor should be realized.[387] An ideal approach – as the IoT is still in the developing stages – would be to generate various models, which are then to be tested for their robustness through the inducement of failures.

The business sector could assist this process by participating in the test. Such participation would allow for technicians to determine exactly how business will be using the IoT and what effect this use can have on the system. Furthermore, the mechanism enables the business sector to comment on various technologies and give their preferences at a very early stage, which may avoid complaints about the IoT at a later stage.

1.2 Availability

Availability of a system is the proportion of time that it is able to be used and the time it takes the system to recover from a failure.[388] Availability is important for any technology. However, for the IoT it is particularly significant because businesses are involved. The limitation of availability may result in logisitical problems related to ordering and supplying the provision of status updates, a cutback in functionality, a production stop, sabotage or reduced transparency. Finally, for the end-user, a lack of availability gives rise to product data not being available, limited functionality of services for "smart offices" or "smart homes", or limited functionality of personal consulting services.[389]

Availability of the IoT is increased if it is decentralized. As the ONS presents itself now, with only one root, the system can suffer from a "single point of failure". If the one existing root is attacked and suffers from a breakdown – e.g. through a denial-of-service attack[390] – the whole IoT is incapacitated. The ideal scenario would allow for roots to intercept queries directed to the attacked root and answer them instead. However, technology may not yet be in the position to configure such a mechanism. Furthermore, it would require that every root has all the data available which is neither realistic nor very practical.

---

[387] KENNEDY, 7.

[388] See BIROLINI, 9; STAVROULAKIS, 72.

[389] Deutsches Bundesministerium für Wirtschaft und Technologie, 23.

[390] See above III.B.1.

The requirement of availability includes the system's capability to accommodate a large number of subscribers. Users need to be able to retrieve information from the IoT without delays. This service has to be guaranteed even if many users are simultaneously inquiring for information, i.e. the service should not be slowed down.

Furthermore, before the tagging of objects is started, the number of possible unique identification numbers has to be determined. It must also be ensured that this number is sufficient to identify all possible objects for at least the mid-term future. In addition, the IoT must be wary so as not to use all possible identifications while the system is in its infancy.[391]

Notwithstanding this fact, an expansion of the IoT may at some time become necessary. Therefore, the system has to be construed in a way that ensures the capability of future expansion, i.e. the long-term sustainability of the IoT must be guaranteed. The IoT should continuously be accessible while the system is transformed or extended, without suffering from a temporary shutdown. This is particularly important as more and more businesses will transfer a large part of their delivery and/or ordering through the IoT and are therefore dependent on the system functioning in order to carry out their daily business.

1.3 Reliability

Reliability of a system is the ability of users thereof to gain confidence in it, i.e. to trust that the system continuously performs and functions in normal as well as in hostile or unexpected circumstances. In more technical terms, "[r]eliability is the probability of a product performing without failure, a specified function under given conditions for a specified period of time."[392]

Measuring the reliability of electronic products first became a discipline in the US during the 1950s due to the increasing complexity of military electronic systems which were failing more and more often. In 1957, the Advisory Group on Reliability of Electronic Equipment (AGREE) defined the term reliability and provided for guidelines to measure and improve reliability.[393] This concept was expanded by the American National Standard Institute (ANSI) and American Society for

391 For example, in the Internet, a transition of Internet Protocol (from IPv4 to IPv6) has become necessary because the current IP addressing system is at risk of not being able to satisfy all IP address requests made by Internet hosts, see WEBER, Internet Governance, 186–202.

392 STAVROULAKIS, 6; see also BIROLINI, 2.

393 AGREE, Reliability of Military Electronics Equipment, AGREE Task Group Report, US, Government Printing Office, Washington, D.C., 1957.

Quality Control (ASQC) to include all products and services and services in 1978.[394]

Whereas in the beginning, reliability was assessed from a provider's view, it has now transformed in a perspective of users. In particular, three components are determinative for users: accessibility of the system,[395] continuity in the delivering of services, and fulfilment of the user's quality expectations.[396]

Reliability can only be measured for each service individually.[397] Therefore, the reliability of the IoT cannot be evaluated as such, but different components of the IoT have to be considered and, thereupon, a comprehensive assessment be carried out. Individual services of the IoT include e.g. the posting of information or the accessibility of information for interested parties.

In practice, reliability can be seen in the task of anticipating the sources of failures or reduced performance of the system, i.e. the disconnection of the network or degraded performance. However, such is not the only aspect of reliability. The consequences of failures or reduced performance are just as important to consider. Mechanisms have to be foreseen for such cases, as well as their practical implementations.

In constructing such mechanisms, the failure source plays an important part. Three different ways of reliability issues may arise: intentional damage, failures caused by extrinsic factors or random failures. Each of these categories requires different responses. In addition, for each foreseeable point of failure, information about services depending on this point has to be available in the hope that the failure can be addressed at an early stage and will not affect all of the depending services.[398]

An approach to produce a reliable system is to create a prototype that is then tested for the three mentioned categories of failures. While, of course, not all failures are foreseeable and issues may arise once the final system is in operation, a prototype nevertheless offers a certain security as the probably most important sources of failure can be found and solutions for them created before the actual system starts its function. However, considering the size and complexity of the IoT, a prototype effective in the discovery of failure sources may be difficult to construct. In particular, it is unlikely that a prototype would be able to take into account the globality and therefore the number of users of the IoT.

---

394 ANSI/ASQC Standard A3–1978, Quality Systems Terminology, American Society for Quality Control, Milwaukee, Wisconsin; see also Stavroulakis, 6.

395 To this aspect see below IV.E.2.

396 Stavroulakis, 14–15.

397 See also Stavroulakis, 7; Birolini, 2.

398 Stavroulakis, 3–4; see also Birolini, 3–4.

In view of this aspect, it is important to note that the IoT will require access[399] from a number of users, who could potentially inquire the IoT for information simultaneously. The system must therefore have the necessary capacities to accommodate any number of users active in the system.

Besides considering potential failures that may arise during the future operation of the IoT, constant monitoring of the system while it is in operation is also necessary to ensure reliability. Failures have to be located and addressed as early as possible. At that point, their sources and reasons should be followed up in order to avoid the same problems occurring again.

1.4 Interoperability

The IoT requires various forms of connectivity and their interoperability. In particular, connectivity has to be established between computers and networks, between users of different computers and networks, between people and things and among things.[400] While connectivity assures that various devices are linked to one another, interoperability refers to the compatibility of the respective parts.[401]

Interoperability needs to be implemented from the initial stage of the IoT onwards; such a test is a requirement for the development of this new system. More difficult is the establishment of future interoperability. The IoT may be used in ways that cannot yet be forseen but that will nevertheless also rely on interoperability. Furthermore, the inclusion of the Internet in the functioning of the IoT may introduce various questions of interoperability, because the Internet itself is a very complex fast-developing technology. Therefore, in the future, developments in either the Internet or the IoT will always have to be communicated to the other system and, in that system, an adaptation to the respective changes will have to be installed. Such a mechanism is very labor-intensive and requires a high degree of communication.

Interoperability of different parts of the IoT requires a certain extent of standardization. Private parties, though, do not always voluntarily agree to conform to standards. Incentives for standardization can be economic. However, incentives are low when the transaction costs of the standards development swamp the benefits or when standardization eliminates competitive advantage.[402] Therefore, economic effects of standardizing mechanisms have to be considered in their establishment.

399 See below IV.E.2.

400 For a decentralized and interoperable system see also above I.B.2.

401 For interoperability for telecommunications see SCHERER, 53–54 and 64–65.

402 PERRITT, Information Superhighway, § 8.3.

Furthermore, backward compatibility is indispensable in a technology such as the IoT. As technologies are constantly evolving and improving, individual parts of that system have to be adaptable to new technologies without requiring replacement. The IoT – at this moment – is still in its infancy and technologies are only now being developed. Therefore, compatibility with older parts is not an issue. However, bearing in mind that the IoT also makes use of the Internet, certain aspects of the IoT have to be construed in a way that they are compatible with older versions of the Internet.

An approach to the interoperability of the IoT is to separate its functionality from its technical implementation, i.e. to integrate a diverse set of technologies into the structure of the IoT. This allows for the application of different solutions to different applications. Furthermore, an infrastructure including various technologies is future-proof, as an infrastructure built with heterogeneity in mind will easily be able to implement newly developed devices and networks.[403]

Interoperability requires that providers of software are able to manufacture products which operate with other systems and programs. This requires interface information, i.e. information about systems and programs of other producers which may be protected by copyright. If the market is dominated by one provider, it may be essential for other providers that their products are compatible with those of the dominant undertaking.[404] If the provider can demonstrate that the supply of information is indispensable to carry on business in the market, and the refusal of it results in a risk of elimination of competition, which may in turn impact the technical development to the prejudice of users, the dominant provider may be forced to supply the necessary information.[405]

2. Providing for Access to Infrastructure

Critical resources in the context of the IoT mainly concern the problem of access to the system. In particular, an equitable and non-discriminatory use of the IoT by all interested businesses should be achieved.

Access to infrastructure encompasses open access to the system, open standards, open source software and widespread availability of access points.[406]

Since access and interconnection are of major importance, particularly for smaller market players, not only the principles but also the details of the framework are

403 HALLER/KARNOUSKOS/SCHROTH, 24.
404 For the essential facilities doctrine see below IV.E.2.
405 JONES/SUFRIN, 572.
406 WEBER, Legal Framework, 96.

significant. The degree of openness in respect of access and interconnection substantially influences the effectiveness of market forces.[407] Increasing entrepreneurial mobility in the information technology value chain will only occur if the use of the IoT is available to all interested persons and enterprises. Interconnection means the physical linking of separate networks (establishment of any-to-any communications); access is a broader concept comprising all requests by market participants to obtain access to a network operator's assets or its users.[408]

Stability, growth and global reach of the IoT require a coordinated development of resources, all of which should reinforce the longstanding custom of openness within the Internet technical community. In particular, open standards and respective transparent policies, which should not be tied to proprietary measures,[409] can have significant positive network effects and make the Internet a powerful communication and collaboration tool.[410] Openness is also in line with the principle of non-discrimination.[411]

An important topic in this context is the affordability of access and its communication possibilities. Relevant aspects are international connectivity prices and costs; reasonable pricing is crucial for the successful implementation of the IoT and for maintaining its end-to-end-functionality. In less developed countries realizing IoT availability and reliability on a cost effective basis is a major issue.[412] In other words, the costs associated with the building of networks and with access aspects as well as the associated revenues are to be distributed among the different players in a fair way.[413]

In addition, root servers need to be available. If possible, root servers should be located in a geographically balanced manner. A number of root servers should be available not only to represent all regions, but also to prevent an overload which would result in a failure of the system.

The right to access can also be seen based on the essential facilities doctrine. The concept emerged in US law and expanded into European law. A number of decisions of the European Commission have lead to the general acceptance of this doctrine, for example as far as the granting of access to some kind of facility or

407 GREWLICH, 145.
408 GREWLICH, 148.
409 See also WEBER, Regulatory Models, 109–112.
410 DORIA/KLEINWÄCHTER, 78.
411 This principle governs international trade rules according to the WTO legal principles.
412 For the digital divide see also below V.A.
413 For access as a scarce resource in the Internet see WEBER, Internet Governance, 205–207.

resource controlled by a dominant undertaking is concerned. A refusal to grant access to an essential facility may be construed as a breach of competition rules.[414]

(i) Essential facilities can be defined as "a facility or infrastructure without access to which competitors cannot provide services to their users".[415] Access by competitors has to be truly "essential" to justify the obligations imposed on the dominant undertaking, and not only desirable.[416] In the future, access to the IoT may become indispensable for businesses to operate. If all information is provided through the IoT, and users buy their products mainly based on this platform, lack of access to the service may determine the death of a company. Therefore, the IoT may be considered an essential facility.

(ii) The European Court of Justice has defined dominance as "a position of economic strength enjoyed by an undertaking which enables it to hinder the maintenance of effective competition on the relevant market by allowing it to behave to an appreciable extent independently of its competitors and users and ultimately of users."[417] Depending on the number of governing bodies and servers providing access, a dominant undertaking may eventually develop in the context of the IoT, which calls into life the essential facilities doctrine.

3. Overcoming Non-technical Barriers

Information made available through the IoT needs to be understood by the users of the framework if the IoT wants to succeed in practice and serve as a global forum for the exchange of goods. However, different languages used all over the world may result in difficulties of communication and, thereby, could prevent users from being informed about products they may be interested in due to linguistic difficulties.

Law, and in particular national legislation, could also impede the technical development of the IoT and its application in practice. In the following, two main as-

414 European Court of Justice, Case C-418/01, IMS Health GmbH & Co. OHG vs. NDC Health GmbH & Co. KG, judgment of April 29, 2004; European Court of Justice, Case C-241/91 P and C-242/91 P, Radio Telefis Eireann (RTE) and Independent Television Publications Ltd. (ITP) v. Commission of the European Communities, judgment of April 6, 1995; Jones/Sufrin, 537–542; Schulz, 65–78; Perritt, Information Superhighway, § 2.20.

415 Sealink/B&I Holyhead: Interim Measures, 1992, 5 CMLR 255.

416 Jones/Sufrin, 542; Gringras, 442.

417 European Court of Justice, Case 322/81, Michelin v. Commission, 1983, E.C.R. 3461, 3503; for the notion of dominance see also Graham, 14–193–14–198; Gringras, 435–438; Schulz, 80–81.

pects are discussed which may emerge as major legal obstacles to the deployment of the IoT.

3.1 Language Barriers

Users have diverse linguistic backgrounds. Hence, for information made available, translations of the relevant documents into at least English are necessary in order to make them understandable for as many people as possible.[418] Whether or not data should be translated into other languages (in particular the six UN languages, i.e. English, French, Spanish, Arabic, Chinese and Russian) depends on the importance of the information and on the frequency of information releases. If the intervals between the different releases of data are short, translating all documents into several languages may not be possible.

Multilingualism is also an issue in the Internet. The Geneva Declaration of Principles stated that "the international management of the Internet would have to be [...], taking into account multilingualism".[419] Furthermore, the same provision on multilingualism has also been included in the Tunis Agenda.[420] At the second Internet Governance Forum (IGF) in Rio de Janeiro in November 2007, multilingualism as a key concept to ensure cultural diversity and participation for all linguistic groups in cyberspace was thoroughly addressed. In particular, the concern that hundreds of local languages may be sidestepped, albeit unintentionally in the radical expansion of Internet communication and information, was addressed.[421]

With regard to the effect of multilingualism on the Internet, two areas have to be considered in particular: multilingual online content and access to such content by the use of domain names that include non-ASCII characters[422] (so-called internationalized domain names,[423] or IDNs).[424] IDNs are at the moment available for use at the second level of the domain system, and the ICANN is actively involved in making these IDNs available at the top level. A multitude of non-ASCII scripts

418 English is the most common programming language; it can therefore be assumed that English is the language that reaches the most people.

419 WSIS, Geneva Declaration of Principles, Article 48.

420 Tunis Agenda for the Information Society, para 29.

421 See http://www.icann.org/en/announcements/announcement-2–13nov07.htm.

422 The American Standard Code for Information Interchange (ASCII) is a character-encoding scheme based on the ordering of the English alphabet. It includes the Roman alphabet (minuscules and capital letters), numbers, and several punctuation marks and control characters.

423 For IDNs see CHEON.

424 See also DORIA/KLEINWÄCHTER, 10 and 13; Internet Society, Briefing Paper: Multilingualism and the Internet, May 14, 2009, available at: http://www.isoc.org/pubpolpillar/docs/multilingualism-20090514.pdf.

are considered, including right-to-left scripts (Arabic being the most widespread) and languages based on non-alphabetic scripts (Mandarin Chinese being the largest thereof).[425]

The ICANN as governing body of the Internet upholds its homepage in English. Its brochure, however, can be downloaded in Arabic, Chinese, English, French, German, Indonesian, Italian, Japanese, Korean, Malaysian, Polish, Portuguese, Russian, Spanish, Swahili, Thai and Vietnamese. Work is in progress to translate all documents into Arabic, English, Spanish, French, Portuguese, Russian and Chinese.[426]

The question of languages has also been addressed in other areas, for example in the environmental field. Obviously, environmental matters concern civil society. After two years of discussions and negotiations, the Aarhus Convention[427] was signed and thereafter put into force. The Convention governs the informational and participatory relations between the authorities and civil society. While the Aarhus Convention does not specifically address linguistic issues, it confirms three pillars depending from each other: (1) access to information, (2) public participation in decision-making, and (3) access to justice. The first two pillars concerning the right to information and participation contain the requirement of multilingualism, which was therefore discussed in the environmental context.

Because businesses are the primary beneficiaries of the IoT, it may be justified to burden them with the task of translating their information. As long as translation is only required into one main language, the benefits from increasing turnover are likely to still outweigh the additional costs of a translating service. Furthermore, these translators will also be needed once contact to interested users has been established and the process of negotiations has started up.

The use of mainly one language is also important for the efficiency of search engines. The establishment of search engines does not easily allow the detection of relevant information in any language. However, if only results are found of information published in the language that the requestor has used, valuable information may not be received. Therefore, at least summaries of the information provided by businesses have to be translated into English. These difficulties may also

425 Twomey, 1.

426 Internet Corporation for Assigned Names and Numbers (ICANN), Proposed Budget: Fiscal Year 2007–2008, May 17, 2007; updated June 29, 2007, available at: http://www.icann.org/financials/adopted-budget-29jun07.htm; for the status of the translations see http://www.icann.org/translations.

427 UN/ECE Convention on Access to Information, Public Participation in Decision Making and Access to Justice, signed in Aarhus, Denmark on June 25, 1998; available at: http://www.unece.org/env/pp/documents/cep43e.pdf.

have to be taken into account when establishing algorithms that determine content relevance of information by search engines.

3.2 Legal Barriers

a) Regulation of Radio Frequency

The RFID as an aspect of the IoT relies on the radio, which is controlled by national regulations. Therefore, allocated bands or the conditions of such use may vary between States.[428]

In Switzerland, the Federal Office for Communication (OFCOM) establishes the national plan of allocation for radio frequencies, which allocates certain frequencies to the one service or several services for use. This plan is approved by the Federal Council.[429] Similar decision-making procedures also apply in other countries.

Radio frequency ranges from 118kHz through to microwave frequencies up to 5.8 GHz, and exceptionally up to 25 GHz.[430] It is important for the IoT that all RFID tags attached to objects operate at the same frequency in order to allow users to effectively use the system. Should different frequencies be installed in different States, the IoT as a platform for the exchange of information becomes impractical.

The International Telecommunication Union (ITU) has established frequency allocations for "Industrial, Scientific and Medical" purposes (ISM bands). These bands are distributed throughout the range of RFID bands. There are regional differences within the ITU system, as well as possibly regional and national frequency allocations differing from the ITU recommendations.[431]

Nevertheless, the efforts seen in this regulatory harmonization can benefit global RFID usage, and potentially, the establishment of specific frequencies for the IoT. Accordingly, bands have to be harmonized and regulated. Such harmonization is necessary to obtain interoperability. It may be best suited for governments to establish a universal frequency for RFID tags that are subsequently used in the IoT. As frequency allocation falls within the autonomy of States, these should also be responsible for handling frequencies for the IoT. Furthermore, States will also

428 CASAGRAS, 54.
429 Art. 3 Verordnung über Frequenzmanagement und Funkkonzessionen, FKV (SR 784.102.1).
430 CASAGRAS, 57.
431 CASAGRAS, 57–58.

have to make sure that the frequencies allocated to RFID tags do not interfere with other services such as radio or television.

b) Health Impacts of the Internet of Things

Opposition to the attribution of all objects with RFID tags could also come from States based on health[432] and safety concerns. RFID tags output electromagnetic energy, the effect of which on human health has not yet been established.

Non-ionizing radiation may affect the human body in a long-term view. Radiation can lead to cells suffering physical, chemical and biological changes. Changes of cells as parts of the individual person will influence the functioning of tissues, organs and systems, and ultimately the organism. Ionizing radiation in particular can be dangerous because of its capacity of producing ions, which are responsible for biological damage in living organisms.[433]

Furthermore, tags may interfere with devices used by individuals for survival, e.g. pacemakers.[434] If such scenarios could in fact realize themselves, human life would be in danger. In addition, the risk of tagged objects interfering with hospital equipment may also be argued by opponents.

Consequently, the effects of the designation of all things with electromagnetic tags have to be considered with respect to health issues. Potential risks need to be identified before the IoT becomes reality, or is rejected based on insufficient studies that do not exhaustively address health risks.

Electromagnetic Fields (EMF) resulting from the tagging of all things have to be measured, which calls for specific tools to detect the said energy. EMF, however, can potentially contaminate the whole environment and interfere in wide frequency range.[435] Therefore, EMF sources and exposure to EMF have to be carefully assessed and monitored.[436]

Furthermore, solutions to potential risks have to be introduced, such as e.g. barriers that intercept radiation. However, such barriers can practically only be installed in specific locations for very specific purposes, for example in hospitals. They are not suitable to protect the individual from negative effects of radiation.

The ITU has issued several recommendations concerning electromagnetic environments effects. The ITU's goal is to give guidance to interested parties, as well

[432] For the positive effects of the IoT on health see below V.E.
[433] BOTELHO/SANTOS/LOPES et al., 67.
[434] VAN DER TOGT/VAN LIESHOUT/HENSBROEK/BEINAT/BINNEKADE/BAKKER, 2887–2888.
[435] BIENKOWSKI, 229.
[436] For EMF measurement methods see BIENKOWSKI, 229–237.

as providing limits for human exposure to electromagnetic fields, Firstly, ITU-T Recommendation K.52 defines classes depending on the category of transmitting antenna directivity, accessibility to people and general public or occupational exposure. A simple equation is given for each class, allowing for compliance evaluation. Secondly, ITU-T Recommendation K.61 gives guidance to measure and numerically predict electromagnetic fields for compliance with human exposure limits for telecommunication installation. Thirdly, ITU-T Recommendation K.70 suggests mitigation techniques to decrease radiation levels in areas around typical transmitting or base stations that are accessible to people. In particular, the Recommendation gives guidance on how to identify the main source of radiation (emitting the highest levels of radiation) as well as the required modification of the transmitting antennas configuration in order to decrease radiation levels.[437]

The International Commission on Non-Ionizing Radiation Protection (ICNIRP) has also issued Guidelines on Limits of Exposure to Static Magnetic Fields.[438] These Guidelines are based on scientific evidence determine exposure limits and suggest protective measures.

Considering the benefits of the IoT in other areas,[439] it is essential that studies are carried out examining effects as well as solutions of the IoT on human health. Otherwise, potentials for global welfare in different areas will be neglected, which in turn would constitute an enormous setback in the practical and beneficial use of new technologies.

The results of these studies and assessments could consequently be transformed into guidelines or – if possible – binding law. In particular, provisions are able to be introduced in existing energy law. Thereby, States would be bound to take measures to protect the general public from the electromagnetic fields emitted by tagged objects. However, possibilities to establish such regulation at the international level have to be explored, as radiation through tagged things has a global impact.

The UN as an organization including almost all States may be the appropriate body to introduce regulation concerning the protection against radiation. Furthermore, the UN itself as well as specialized agencies of the UN without legal personality, have already dealt with international energy law, thereby possessing a knowledge basis that may put them in the position to effectively deal with the issue. In particular, the UN Environment Program (UNEP) comes to mind.[440] Created in 1972, the UNEP's function was to act as a focal point for environmental

437 See Lewicki, 244–245.

438 See http://www.icnirp.de/documents/statgdl.pdf.

439 See below V.

440 For the UNEP see Birnie/Boyle/Redgwell, 65–71.

action and coordination within the UN system. The UNEP's program had seven priorities, i.e. human settlements and habitats, health of people and their environment, terrestrial ecosystems and their management and control, environment and development, oceans, energy, and natural disasters.[441] Under the heading of health of people and their environment, protection against radiation could be included in the UNEP's program.

However, the UNEP has been suffering from major difficulties in the past few years. In particular, the program has not been able to keep up with the latest developments. Furthermore, it has encountered financial difficulties, absence of focus, problems of location and management difficulties.[442] Nevertheless, the UNEP has also celebrated some successes and has the ability to contribute to the development and implementation of international environmental policy if the mentioned difficulties are addressed. The UNEP has helped the international community in the creation and expansion of several international treaties, and has thereby served as a catalyst for international environmental cooperation. Such action is, once again, necessary to address the issue discussed in this chapter.

The newly emerging issues that are brought forth by the IoT may serve as a chance for the UNEP to rethink the difficulties that have obstructed its work in the past and creating new mechanisms to address the issue of radiation at the international level.

441 Downie/Levy, 356.
442 Downie/Levy, 357–362.

V. Internet of Things as Tool of Global Welfare

The IoT has the potential to increase global welfare in various ways. Below, a few examples are listed and ideas developed. However, the mentioned applications are not conclusive.

A. Bridging the Digital Divide

1. Introduction

The problem of a digital divide has already arisen in the context of other information technologies, in particular the Internet. So far, however, there is no single general abstract definition of the digital divide; [443] it encompasses a wide spectrum of disparities and differences based on manifold factors. It is also a dynamic concept, which evolves over time. Broadly speaking, the perceived gap which surfaced between those who have access to information technology and those who do not, is referred to with the concept of digital divide.[444]

The term originated as a catch-phrase in US national studies of inequalities regarding access to information and communication.[445] Afterwards, it quickly became so familiar that it entered every day political and societal debates. Mostly, the digital divide is understood as the "uneven diffusion of information and communication technology".[446] The digital divide could also be understood through the closely-linked mirror-inverted concept of "digital opportunity". Information technology is no longer a luxury, but a development tool.[447]

Bridging the digital divide is a matter of social justice encompassing not only access to information and communication networks, but also dimensions of life from health care and nutrition to education and longevity.[448] Enabling civil society in all countries to participate in the exchange of information and communication means acquiring soft power, being the ability to achieve desired outcomes through

443 This chapter is based on WEBER, Internet Governance, 248–264.

444 For further details see WEBER/MENOUD, Digital Divide, 4.

445 See survey of the National Telecommunications and Information Administration (NTIA): Falling Through the Net: Defining the Digital Divide, Doc. SIN 003-000-00687-5, Washington D.C. 1999, available at: http://www.ntia.doc.gov/ntiahome/fttn99/; see also YU, 2–3 with further references.

446 UNITED NATIONS DEVELOPMENT PROGRAM (UNDP), Making New Technologies Work for Human Development, Human Development Report 2001, New York/Oxford 2001, 38.

447 See YU, 16.

448 NORRIS, 49.

R.H. Weber and R. Weber, *Internet of Things*, DOI 10.1007/978-3-642-11710-7_5,

attraction rather than coercion.[449] Soft power works by convincing others "to follow or getting them to agree to norms and institutions that produce the desired behavior".[450] Substantively, soft power depends on the persuasiveness of the free information that an actor seeks to transmit.

With regard to the IoT, it is in particular the gap between developed and developing countries that is at issue. However, divides between different levels of education of individuals is less important for the IoT than it is for the Internet, because the IoT will mainly be used by enterprises.

2. Importance of the Digital Divide in the IoT

Information and communication networks create opportunities for electronic business expressions by individuals, groups and enterprises which otherwise would not have media access.[451] Compared with the traditional news media, the Internet, the IoT and other new communication technologies provide a more level playing field for what ever kind of competition, thus increasing the leverage of small and emerging parties.[452] Experience during the last few years has shown that members of civil society will want to be able to move in and out of different types of networks depending on which one is most appropriate to their needs at a given time.[453]

A lack of participation possibilities for all members of civil society would also pose a certain danger to democracy and self-government, thereby compromising individual freedom.[454] In such a situation, a fragmentation of society can occur which potentially undermines social stability.[455] Since a natural human tendency exists to make choices with respect to information and communication that do not disturb the pre-existing view of the world, an increase in polarization caused by the ability of digital technologies to customize may lead to extremism and violence.[456] Even if some doubts can be raised whether indeed all members of civil society would be close-minded and ignorant of the needs for diverse opinions and competing viewpoints, it cannot be overlooked that the digital divide concerns the availability of relevant content and that restrictions related to free access to the

449 KEOHANE/NYE, 220.
450 KEOHANE/NYE, 220.
451 YU, 25.
452 NORRIS, 156.
453 MUELLER, Telecommunications, 659.
454 SUNSTEIN, Republic.com, 192.
455 SUNSTEIN, Republic.com, 194.
456 SUNSTEIN, Republic.com, 57 and 199; see also SUNSTEIN, Deliberative Trouble.

information and communication networks could "customize" some persons out of the content needed to make rational decisions.[457]

The IoT provides for new opportunities in favor of developing countries for the insertion of their goods into global chains. With the use of the IoT, it would be easier for companies situated in developing countries to compete in the global market, since they could post information about their goods in a globally accessible network – a possibility introduced with the IoT.

Furthermore, the shipping of goods from developing countries to other (developed or developing) countries could easily be followed and users would be in the position to constantly know at which stage of the transportation the ordered product is at a specific moment. This mechanism helps to avoid the loss of goods during transport or – if such occurs – the good can easily be localized through the RFID tag.

However, this possibility can only be realized if companies in developing countries dispose of the necessary technologies to access the IoT. The span of required factors is very wide, ranging from electricity to computers and access to the Internet to more specific equipment such as the RFID-tagging of objects. In addition, companies must also be made aware of these new possibilities created through the IoT.

The digital divide needs to be addressed at an international level. Efforts are to be taken in order to overcome the gap among individuals, households, businesses and geographic areas at different socio-economic levels with regard both to their opportunities to access and to make use of the IoT.[458]

Technologies concerned by distribution disparities are manifold and encompass various devices, such as computers, Internet connections and digital switches. Consequently, the bridging of the access divide should encompass the filling of all technological gaps deserving public policy attention.

With regard to the digital divide in the Internet and the there existing technological gap, PETER K. YU discusses five key prerequisites for bridging the digital divide:[459]

- *Awareness:* Those who are not aware of the Internet and of the new communication technologies and those who are not aware of the benefits of computers and online access will not be able to benefit from the chances created by the

457 YU, 49.

458 See OECD, Understanding the Digital Divide, Paris 2001, available at: http://www.oecd.org/dataoecd/38/57/1888451.pdf.

459 YU, 8–16.

new communication possibilities and to take advantage of the digital opportunities.

- *Access:* For obvious reasons, access to the Internet and the new communication technologies is paramount to survive personally and professionally, for example in view of daily communications, business transactions, entertainment, education, job search, research and information gathering, medical assistance and political participation; the Internet has also created many unprecedented opportunities for people with disabilities.[460]
- *Affordability:* In many less developed countries, the costs of hardware and software as well as the interconnection fees are so high that Internet access remains out of reach for many people; the monthly income can certainly not be fully spent on using the Internet.
- *Availability:* Even if having Internet access, many people might not be able to find the information that is relevant to their lives and communities, i.e. to obtain the actually relevant information. An additional barrier to digital participation is language, even if the decision of ICANN of June 2008, to introduce other languages aside from English might have mitigated the problem to a certain extent; at least indigenous people who do not use written language cannot take advantage of Internet access.[461]
- *Adaptability:* Access to information technology and Internet content is useful only if people are able to adapt to the changing technological environment and to use the new technological tools effectively. Computer illiteracy, technophobia, and cyberphobia have posed significant barriers to participation in the online world.[462]

These requirements apply for the IoT as they do for the Internet. However, a difference can be seen in the fact that the IoT, unlike the Internet, will be used mainly by businesses (at least at the beginning). Whereas companies situated in developed countries are likely to meet the prerequisites mentioned above, (usually smaller) companies in less developed countries will need support in establishing an infrastructure through which they can participate in the IoT.

460 See also above IV.E.2.
461 See also above IV.E.3.1.
462 See Yu, 15–16.

3. Financing Strategies

3.1 Financing Needs and Mechanisms

The main factor causing the divide is wealth. Financing strategies are to be discussed to allow all interested parties to participate in the IoT, regardless of their country of origin.

Estimating the level of investment needed to achieve this goal is difficult, particularly due to the high complexity and the variety of components involved. Sufficient basic infrastructures need to be built, including various elements. Furthermore, these establishments have to be adaptable to new innovations and progress in order not to render services obsolete within a short time span, which significantly increases infrastructure costs.[463]

The first step when establishing a financing strategy is necessarily to identify the areas that need additional financing. This implies carrying out a survey of local existing and missing facilities and needs in order to assess where the private sector alone has not provided for adequate funding. Such areas are typically backbone expansion, interconnectivity development, services to low income and remote populations, broadband and human resource capacities, as well as content and applications building.[464]

Even though the IoT is to be established primarily for the private sector, the business sector alone is unlikely to be able to answer the financing needs of the world alone. The public sector should support the bridging of the digital divide, for example by providing the enabling environment and basic conditions (e.g. ensuring the availability of electricity). Furthermore, the promotion of growth of the IoT also addresses the international community.[465]

The support of less-developed countries in the establishment of IoT infrastructure has to be approached by the business sector, the public sector and the international community together. Only such cooperation can effectively lead to global access to the IoT. Whereas the public sector should be primarily responsible for providing its country with the necessary basic requirements (such as electricity), the international community is best suited to increase the availability of computers and Internet access worldwide. This is an extremely difficult and complex task and therefore asks for international commitment. Finally, the business sector

463 For financial strategies in the digital divide of the Internet see WEBER, Internet Governance, 252–253.

464 For financial mechanisms in the digital divide of the Internet see WEBER, Internet Governance, 260.

465 See also WEBER, Internet Governance, 253–254.

could provide IoT-specific equipment to companies in developing countries. As the business sector is most involved in the IoT, it is the sector with the best knowledge on what exactly is needed and how it should be provided to developing countries and be installed there.

These three levels of support to developing countries can be demonstrated in a table as follows:

Levels	Tasks	Responsible Actor
1	Basic requirements (e.g. electricity)	Governments
2	Computers and Internet Access	International Community
3	IoT services	Business Sector

Besides these provisions to developing countries, education of people in developing countries is also of utmost importance. It needs to be ensured that technical support will not have to be kept up, but that businesses in the respective country will be able to follow the developments of the IoT and adapt to the resulting changes by themselves. Concrete instruments can include technical cooperation or improvement of capacity building.

Various approaches to gain funds for certain projects already exist. In the framework of the Internet, a Digital Solidarity Fund (DSF) has been implemented. The DSF was officially inaugurated as the "Digital Solidarity Fund Foundation"[466] – a foundation constituted under Swiss Law with legal domicile in Geneva – on March 14, 2005. The DSF was acknowledged in the second phase of the WSIS in Tunis. Consequently, the DSF was recognized and given political support by several international institutions. At the second World Summit of Cities and Local Authorities on the Information Society, held in Bilbao from November 9 to 11, 2005, the DSF project was officially endorsed. The outcome of the WSIS consisted in a Declaration and in a Preliminary Plan of Action outlining the main political commitments and courses of action agreed on by the participating cities, local and regional authorites. Furthermore, the DSF was also addressed at the occasion of specific conferences on innovative financing for development.[467] However, in October 2009, the suspension of the Fund was decided due to managerial

[466] In French: „Fondation Fonds de Solidarité Numérique".
[467] WEBER/MENOUD, Digital Divide, 147–149.

and administrative reasons. The establishment of a new fund is considered based on clear regulations determining the role of the involved persons.[468]

Nevertheless, in principle, the DSF appears to be a valuable approach to bridging the digital divide and is therefore explained in the following. The DSF aimed at reducing Southern countries' problems with interconnection, infrastructure and training, partly through investments in the South, financed by countries of the North, and partly through increased South-South cooperation. As a concrete mechanism to transfer resources from developed countries to developing ones, the establishment of a "digital snake" was proposed. Hereby, countries whose Internet rate is situated in the upper fluctuation margin of the snake help countries lying outside the snake to meet the lower margin limit by engaging in specified quantified action. Besides voluntary donations, the 1% digital solidarity principle – also known as Geneva principle – consists in a clause that can be inserted in a contract on ICT goods or services, providing that a seller or service provider must transfer 1% of the total transaction value to the Digital Solidarity Fund Foundation. This easy to implement clause is meant primarily for public institutions.[469]

While the DSF-concept of investments in the South by the North and increased South-South cooperation is also applicable for the IoT, the introduction of a 1% clause is more problematic. However, public procurement has a secondary function in serving a competitive environment and ensures that conditions of competition are not distorted, in particular by improving market information (i.e. transparency).[470] Therefore, the introduction of a clause affecting public institutions can hardly be considered unfair or harming users, and does not constitute an obstacle for residual competition.[471]

The DSF is not the only proposal to achieve the funding of a certain goal. Airlines increasingly levy a tax on flight fares which is collected to compensate for carbon offsetting.[472] Users can choose to pay a tax in addition to the flight ticket, which is allotted to a fund. This fund supports environmental projects that help reduce the release of greenhouse gases. Thereby, the levied tax is a contribution to sustainable travel. However, up to now, these initiatives are mainly voluntary.

---

468 See http://www.lequotidien.sn/index.php?option=com_content&task=view&id=10536&Itemid=10.

469 For further details on the DSF see WEBER/MENOUD, Digital Divide, 147–177; WEBER/MENOUD, Digital Solidarity Clause.

470 WEBER/MENOUD, Digital Solidarity Clause, 488–489.

471 WEBER/MENOUD, Digital Solidarity Clause, 491.

472 For example, a passenger flying from Stockholm to New York with the airline SAS would have to pay approximately 20 Euros to offset the carbon dioxide released by the air travel; see http://www.thestar.com/Business/article/191841.

The approach of levying a tax could cause problems in view of the fair competition principle in case of the IoT, where participants are private businesses. Obliging private actors to make a contribution to a fund (thereby possibly reducing the number of competitors) risks to introduce competition restrictions, in particular because 1% of the transaction fee in practice eventually amounts to a considerable sum. However, the approach is not of a discriminatory nature; in addition, it can be argued on an ethical basis that those participants benefiting from the IoT might be charged with contributions in return. Furthermore, private businesses can help in the establishment of the necessary infrastructure in developing countries. Companies making use of the IoT still have to prove their competitiveness in the market.

Another factor in this consideration concerns the fact that businesses in developed countries can contribute to their public image by supporting less-developed countries. It is possible that potential customers are more likely to buy products from companies they know "care about others".

Finally, a third argument for the business sector's contributions towards a fund is that not only does competition increase if business from developing countries can access the IoT, but companies in developed countries, through the information provided from developing countries, might also increase their knowledge about production of goods as well as import and export.

Another approach to fund the support of developing countries would be to introduce an access fee to the IoT for businesses situated in developed countries. The amount of a respective fee could for example be based on the company's turnover. Considering the total amount of the private sector's turnover, such fees would likely cover the costs of support to developing countries. Furthermore, as the business sector will also financially benefit from using the IoT, the introduction of an access fee can be justified. Nevertheless, such a fee can only be introduced based on a respective legal provision.

3.2 Legal Framework of Financial Strategies

An international agreement would achieve the best legal quality if it is adopted by sovereign States or international organizations within the scope of their competences; such agreements are legally binding. However, experience in other fields (e.g. the Internet) has shown that it could be quite difficult to establish and actually implement international binding agreements and that such an approach is usually rather time-consuming.[473]

[473] For the Internet see WEBER, Internet Governance, 263.

Furthermore, the importance of "soft law" should not be underestimated since it has a special legal relevance in the field of good faith and with regard to the interpretation of international law.[474] "Soft law" can also play a major role in legal orders' development. Self-regulation in particular, has the advantage that rules created by the participants of a specific community are usually efficient because they respond to real needs and mirror the technology available; meaningful self-regulation also provides the opportunity to adapt the legal framework to changing technologies in a flexible way. It is also usually possible to implement it at reduced costs (cost-saving effects), and effective measures may induce concerned parties to be open to a permanent consultation process.[475]

Nevertheless, self-regulation is (if at all) only mandatory for States or businesses that participate in them. However, as businesses may not be inclined to join according initiatives, a certain binding framework would be desirable. Decreasing the digital divide before the IoT gains further momentum would also ensure that more businesses and users can participate from the beginning. Therefore, it would be desirable if States or international organizations established a binding regulatory framework, which could then be specified by self-regulatory mechanisms developed by e.g. the business sector or non-governmental organizations (NGOs). If such results cannot be achieved, it would be worthwhile to think of a new self-regulatory body starting the activities on an informal and private law based framework and to consider an eventual "conversion" of this structure into a set of international binding rules at a later stage.

If the idea of introducing an access fee to the IoT is followed up, a law as basis has to be adopted. Only a law can justify the levy of a tax. This law would have to describe how the respective tax is composed, as well as determine who shall be responsible to collect the taxes and transfer them to the fund for assistance to developing countries. Furthermore, exceptions to the levy of a tax also have to be foreseen for companies situated in developed countries.[476] In addition, provisions have to be established that oblige businesses situated in developing countries to pay the respective tax if they are in the position to do so and are not qualified as being in need of support.

4. Outlook

Bridging the digital divide in the IoT – to achieve a global exchange of information about objects – requires the participation and involvement of all actors. On

474 See above II.B.2.

475 See above II.B.

476 For example if the respective company pursues a humanitarian aim.

the one hand, financial aid has to be provided to developing countries. On the other hand, technical cooperation and capacity building should increase the knowledge in developing countries so that future adaptations can be made without additional international support.

Awareness, access, affordability, availability and adaptability are requirements for bridging the digital divide. Without these factors, the inclusion of businesses in developing countries cannot be successful.

Businesses in developed countries, States as well as the international community have to cooperate to establish the necessary infrastructure in developing countries. Each of these three actors should have their own responsibilities and do part of the work for global access to the IoT. Considering the financial side, an approach similar to the DSF for the Internet seems promising. However, it would mainly be based on the cooperation and ethical conscience of the business sector.

While self-regulation has proven to be the most successful mechanism dealing with changing technological environments in the past, it is not entirely sufficient as to regulate the bridging of the digital divide. Some kind of binding legal framework (established best at the international level) would be necessary in order to ensure adherence to mechanisms. If such an approach is not realizable, efforts must be directed to have self-regulatory mechanisms developed into law.

B. Implementing Search Engines

1. Need for Search Engines

Search engines can be described as a fully automated, IT-supported processes, in which providers do not manually intervene.[477] Search engines allow for users to find information by introducing keywords, which results in a list of links to sites that include the requested information. In particular, the use of search engines allows for more control for the user in performing a search.[478]

Information about things will be fragmented across the IoT. Information may be provided at class-level for information of things in the same class, or at serial-level for information that is unique to a particular thing. Furthermore, information may also be provided authoritatively by the producer of the thing or else by other

[477] WEBER, Suchmaschinen, 29; for the architecture of a search engine see LEVENE, 66–69.
[478] MEGHABGHAB/KANDEL, 9.

entities which have, for example, interacted with a particular object at some stage in its life.[479]

This fragmentation asks for a lookup or referral service linking things to information and securing safe and confidental access to the respective business information.[480] Search engines enable users of the IoT to find and access the requested information in a short time span. Such a service will increase the benefits of the IoT for all users, but in particular unexperienced users will heavily rely on the use of search engines. Without search engines, the IoT or the information available through the IoT, respectively, may become unaccessible for a large part of the user base. For individuals as well as small or medium-sized companies, who may not be using the IoT on a regular basis, support in the searching of information is indispensable.

Search engines act as intermediaries, because users do not have the time and/or knowledge to search for the requested information in all sources of information. However, information overload has to be avoided, as such overload can ask too much from the user, who may lose content-oversight. Therefore, resources have to be put in place sensibly.[481] The optimum of information should be provided to the user by search engines,[482] not the maximum of information.[483]

Information retrieval can be illustrated as follows:

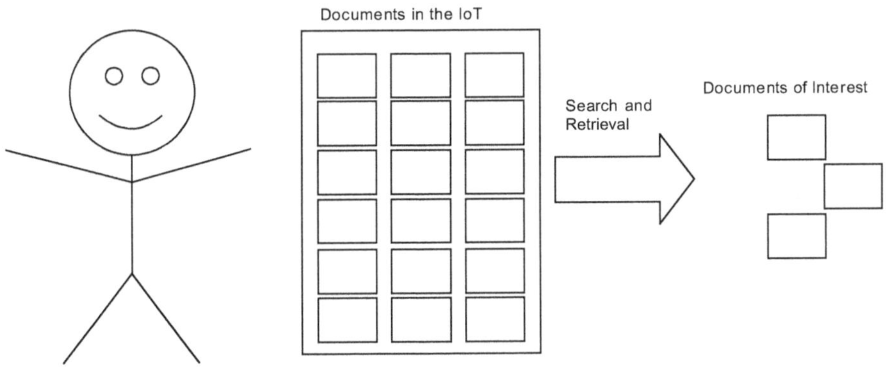

479 European Commission, Strategic Research Roadmap, para. 3.9.
480 European Commission, Strategic Research Roadmap, para. 3.9.
481 DRUEY, 382–383.
482 DRUEY, 70.
483 See also WEBER, Suchmaschinen, 23–25; MEGHABGHAB/KANDEL, 7–8; for the indexing and ranking by search engines in particular and the resulting bias of search engines see GOLDMAN.

Furthermore, things may also require to discover the existence and identity of peer things, with which they want to negotiate about shared goals (such as transportation, storage or handling), as well as to identify and resolve conflicts, thereby achieving efficient, synergistic and considerate solutions for all involved things with regard to co-location and co-transportation.[484]

Finally, a search engine might increase globally accessible information about reviews, ratings, recommendations, tips and advice or information about the availability of new services, updates, and extensions or capabilities for specific classes of things (e.g. software or firmware).[485]

Users should be able to trust the matching between requests and supplies of information.[486] This trust requires particular expertise of search engines of the IoT and its functioning.[487] Search engines can only gain the trust – and therewith the necessary usage of the service – if they can demonstrate to the user that they have an extensive knowledge of the platform and that their service is reliable.

2. Search Engines in the Internet

Lessons for the introduction of search engines in the IoT could be drawn from search engines in the Internet (e.g. Google, Yahoo). These existing search engines would have to be enhanced and adapted to the needs of the IoT.

2.1 Functioning of Search Engines

Before users can insert terms into search engines to retrieve information, search engines have to gather information about webpages from around the loT. This collection of data then has to be processed in such a way that a page's relevance to a particular set of keywords can be determined. This process of determining the content relevance[488] has in practice the same effect as a selection, because users are most likely to only follow up on the first few hits listed by the search engine.[489] Finally, the input by the user is matched to the search engine's database and a list of results delivered to the user.[490]

484 European Commission, Strategic Research Roadmap, para. 3.9.
485 European Commission, Strategic Research Roadmap, para. 3.9.
486 European Commission, Strategic Research Roadmap, para. 3.9; see also Brewer, 54.
487 Weber, Suchmaschinen, 26.
488 On content relevance see Levene, 78–90.
489 Wolling, 17.
490 Halavais, 14–20; Grimmelmann, 7–11; see also Brewer, 53.

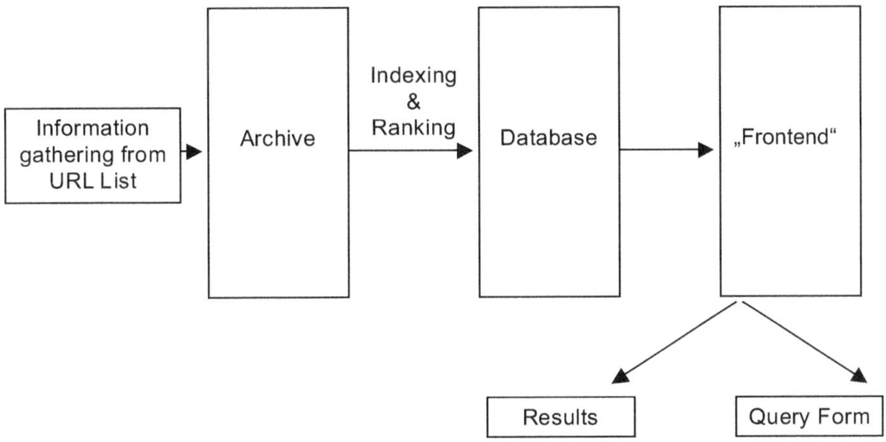

Because each search engine can only produce one section of the information accessible through the IoT, several search engines would have to be used by the requestor of information if he/she wants his/her search to be as outstretched as possible. This procedure, however, might be very cumbersome.[491]

An alternative to search engines in the traditional sense are Meta-Crawlers, inquiring information through a uniform search mask, but using several search engines and presenting an overall list of results to the user. Meta-Crawler does not have its own database, but instead draws its results from the databases of the individual search engines.[492] This approach makes it much easier for the user to achieve the best possible results. Furthermore, it prevents any undesirable influences that may be introduced by the search engines themselves[493] in the lists of results.

2.2 Financing of Search Engines

In this context, the question emerges how search engines are financed. Different scenarios include the introduction of a user fee, a registration fee for businesses, or advertising paid for by businesses on the webpage of the search engine.[494]

The introduction of user fees to search for information in the IoT does not seem sensible. Enterprises will want to make available the information on their products to as many people as possible, in order to generate business. However, if in-

491 Weber, Suchmaschinen, 29.
492 Weber, Suchmaschinen, 29–30.
493 See below V.B.4.
494 Wolling, 16; for advertising in particular see Grimmelmann, 12–13.

terested persons have to pay a fee before accessing the respective information, they may be inclined to pass on the opportunities provided by the IoT, which in turn results in losses for the business sector.

Advertising on the pages of search engines is not ideal, either, as it may distract users with unwanted information. Mainly larger businesses have the financial capabilities to pay for advertising and thereby enlarge their user base. Nevertheless, it has to be kept in mind that advertising is a legitimate opportunity for business to generate income. Furthermore, advertising – especially on sites frequently visited – may provide a large amount of income for search engines, which allows for engines to improve their functioning. This in turn benefits the user.

At last, registration fees for businesses may be introduced. On the one hand, this approach is justified because, in the end, companies benefit from users being directed to their information and potentially buying their products or services. However, registration fees may also prevent (especially smaller) companies from accessing the IoT, which limits the achievement of the goal of the IoT to serve as a global platform for the exchange of goods.

Therefore, while considering the disadvantages of advertising on the sites of search engines, this approach seems to be the most appropriate (or least hurtful) financing mechanism for search engines.

2.3 Liability of Search Engines

Liability of search engines may emerge in cases of violations of data protection or competition laws.

In the Internet, liability of search engines has been based on either a paid or a non-paid legal relationship between the search engine and the user, provider of information or advertiser. Furthermore, tortuous liability could also be established, or special concepts of liability may be applied (such as product liability or disturbance liability).[495] Claims would be based on national laws on liability.

On the one hand, it is impossible for search engines to verify the information in the IoT they provide or to ensure they do not violate the privacy of individuals.[496] If such information turns out to be incorrect, or products defective, the company manufacturing them should be held liable according to conventional liability law.

495 WEBER, Suchmaschinen, 155–165.

496 See GRIMMELMANN, 40.

On the other hand, if search engines violate data protection or competition laws, they themselves have to be held liable. The most convenient approach would be to establish a special liability regime for search engines in the IoT. Such a regime, however, is unlikely to be adopted in time. Therefore, general liability bases need to be applied.

The relationship between the search engine and the complaining party has to be determined. Based on this determination, jurisdiction and applicable law can be appointed. The requirements to prove liability are described by the respective domestic laws.

Grokster[497] teaches the requirements to claim secondary copyright liability.[498] Grokster consisted of a search application fused with a file-transfer application, which makes the guidelines applicable directly to search engines.[499] First, manufacturers and distributers of technology are not liable for infringements committed by its users as long as the technology also has substantial noninfringing uses.[500] Second, manufacturers must not have acted with the intent of inducing its users to infringe.[501] These guidelines can also be applied to the IoT as the problems in the IoT largely correspond to the problems in the Internet. Accordingly, search engines easily pass the test of substantial noninfringing uses. However, specifics concering purposeful, culpable inducement by search engines have not yet been pronounced.[502]

3. Position of Search Engines in the Market Place

Under most national laws (including Swiss law), search engines are not subject of authorization by the State.[503] They can operate freely and do not have to apply for accreditation or have to pay for a concession.

Because market access barriers are usually relatively low for electronic service offerings, the installation of certain connections is not very time-consuming or expensive. However, due to the dynamics of events in electronic markets, it may

497 MGM Studios, Inc. v. Grokster, Ltd., 545 U.S. 913, 2005.

498 For search engine liability for copyright infringements see also FITZGERALD/O'BRIEN/FITZGERALD.

499 MGM Studios, Inc. v. Grokster, Ltd., 545 U.S. 913, 2005, 921.

500 This principle was already introduced in Sony Corp. v. Universal City Studios, Inc., 464 U.S. 417, 1984, 456.

501 MGM Studios, Inc. v. Grokster, Ltd., 545 U.S. 913, 2005, 935; see also FITZGERALD/O'BRIEN/FITZGERALD, 4.

502 GRIMMELMANN, 34.

503 WEBER, Suchmaschinen, 37–38.

be difficult to achieve a market-leading position.[504] Furthermore, there are certain market barriers in electronic markets that have only very little significance in traditional markets. In particular, it may be difficult to achieve sufficient name recognition in order to acquire an appropriate market share which is necessary for economic survival. This requirement presupposes an enormous effort in advertising, which cannot be activated in the balance sheet. Furthermore, such expenses are needed at the beginning of business activities, where liquid assets are limited. In addition to advertising, the collection of information to establish a database is also very expensive.[505]

Companies themselves may be interested in developing such search engines, as these may increase business, thereby increasing the profits of the company. However, if such is the case, particular attention has to be paid to the fact that companies respect the principles of fair competition and treat all information equally, rather than privileging information on their own products.

4. Fair Competition

Search engines have to respect the principles of fair competition in their operation.[506] This is particularly important within the IoT, where businesses disperse their information in order to access potential new users.

Search engines should display all offers matching a specific keyword, and must not discriminate against particular businesses. Furthermore, search engines should not be allowed to conclude agreements in which companies agree to financially contribute, and the search engine preference products of the respective producer.

In order to ensure that not only particular information is displayed, search engines could disclose their underlying algorithms in a full and truthful manner. Such disclosure would provide for transparency for users.[507] However, in practice such a mechanism may – in the end – not benefit the user, as businesses could use the respective information to understand the ranking mechanism and thereby try to artificially "manipulate" the rankings to their advantage.[508]

Nevertheless, principles of fair competition need to be introduced for search engines as they are already in existence in the business sector. Violations of the respective provisions may then lead to fines and/or reparations.

---

504 WEBER, Suchmaschinen, 112.
505 WEBER, Suchmaschinen, 112–113.
506 See also GRIMMELMANN, 27–30.
507 For the need of transparency of search engines see also GOLDMAN, 194.
508 LEVENE, 58–59.

C. Combating Product Counterfeiting

The attribution of objects with an RFID tag could allow for the control of the authenticity of products. Therefore, an organization would have to be appointed with the task to control that only authentic products are attributed with a tag. Consequently, counterfeited products would not be able to enter the supply chain, which represents a mechanism to discourage counterfeiting.

Already in 2006, the drug company Pfizer began using RFID to combat drug counterfeiting in the US. Pfizer started the experiment on the drug Viagra, which is the drug most often counterfeited in the US. Passive high-frequency RFID tags are attached to the drug package, which allows the company to follow up on the drugs until they arrive in pharmacies. An RFID device interrogator then encodes an EPC to each tag, before a second interrogator verifies that the tag has been successfully encoded and can be read. Furthermore, the RFID interrogator reads the unique number stored in the tag, enabling Pfizer to record both the identity of the tag and the item's EPC in a database.

The automated tagging process was developed by Pfizer in collaboration with Systech, a provider of automated packaging and data collection systems. Subsequently, pharmacists can use the tags to authenticate the drug over the Internet. SupplyScape, a Woburn (Mass.), creator of pharmaceutical supply chain software, provides an online service to which pharmacists and wholesalers must subscribe. If the EPC was not issued by Pfizer, or the identity of the tag does not match the one stored in the database, the pharmacist or wholesaler is put on notice and asked to quarantine the product. Furthermore, Pfizer's Medical Information Services, a group of Pfizer employees who process suspected cases of counterfeit drugs, is also informed and will likely ask the pharmacist or wholesaler to send the suspected Viagra back to Pfizer for investigation.[509]

The use of RFID as a means of authenticating and tracking drugs throughout the supply chain has also been endorsed by the US Food and Drug Administration.

The World Intellectual Property Organization (WIPO) would be an appropriate organization to fulfil this task.[510] The WIPO disposes of an extensive knowledge in the area of intellectual property rights. Furthermore, it meets the requirement of globality of the IoT. Currently, 184 States are members of the WIPO, i.e. over 90 percent of the countries of the world. In addition, the WIPO also works with a wide spectrum of international organizations, NGOs, as well as representatives of the civil society and industry groups. Some 250 NGOs and international organi-

[509] See http://www.rfidjournal.com/article/articleview/2075/1/1/.

[510] For the WIPO see MAY.

zations have observer status at WIPO meetings.[511] The inclusion of the private sector is appropriate for the IoT; it is important that the business sector gets a voice in the determination of policies. With the WIPO's involvement in disputes relating to the Internet and electronic commerce (in particular disputes arising out of abusive registration and use of Internet domain names),[512] the organization has also shown its capability to adapt to new technologies.

Furthermore, the WIPO Arbitration and Mediation Center[513] could be used for the settlement of disputes if and when such arise. With regard to the IoT, in particular non-contractual disputes (e.g. patent infringements) come to mind. The WIPO Arbitration and Mediation Center provides of the necessary knowledge in intellectual property disputes and its understanding of new technologies, it is also an appropriate body to handle disputes arising in the IoT.

D. Tackling Environmental Concerns

1. Sustainable Environment Policies

The use of IoT technologies not only allows for monitoring and statistics' collection but has also the potential to provide powerful tools in the fight against climate change. Through the IoT, current and historic data can be managed and processed, improving environmental performance. Unlike the inconsistent, unstructured and not always reliable data of today, the database made of the data collected through sensors would allow the public and private sector to take informed decisions on how to improve their environmental performance and put together strategies for a "greener" economy.[514] However, such improvement requires for the collected data (and potentially also forecasts based on that data) to be publicly available.

Furthermore, the monitoring of environments through sensor technologies could warn of natural disasters (e.g. volcanic eruptions, floods), thereby avoiding a loss of life through evacuation of residents in locations at risk. In addition, sensors may stop accidental emissions which e.g. pollute water by detecting the emission and communicating with the next valve in the sewer to block the pollutant in progress.[515] Sensors may also be used to prevent the loss of human life in (former)

[511] See http://www.wipo.int/about-wipo/en/how_wipo_works.html.
[512] See also WEBER, Information Society, 30–33; MAY, 56–61.
[513] See http://www.wipo.int/amc/en/.
[514] Amcham EU, 7.
[515] EPoSS, 23.

conflict zones. For example, special robots have been used for mine detection in countries like India, Thailand and Turkey.[516]

Sensor networks using smart systems communications technology or mobile robots of the future can also be used in networked systems that are placed in inaccessible or remote locations such as oil platforms, mines, forest, tunnels, and pipes. These sensors may assist in preventing, detecting and correcting dangerous situations by alarming the responsible authorities in case of changes in the environment.[517]

In a nutshell, it can be said that the advance provided through the IoT over today's situation lies in the distributed control, which offers faster and more cost efficient responses than what is achievable with centralized monitoring and control.[518]

2. Energy Consumption

The IoT, through the tagging of objects, can improve traffic and travel planning and thereby reduce emissions. The system should enable travelers to find out the best way to get from point A to point B by using all the available options, which include private and public transportation. Furthermore, information could be transmitted through tags about traffic jams, accidents, road works etc. to avoid travelers using blocked roads.[519]

However, the IoT does not only have the potential of helping to improve the environmental performance in traveling. Using "smart objects" would also assist in lowering the consumption of energy in private households. For example, the use of sensors in houses could allow for a dynamic adjusting of room temperature and lighting – saving energy by automatically turning off the heat or lights.[520]

However, while the IoT provides for possibilities to decrease the consumption of scarce resources as well as to improve environmental performance, these possibilities by themselves do not create any obligations. Therefore, the use of the respective opportunities rests on the ecological conscience of individuals and pos-

516 ITU, 11.

517 EPoSS, 24.

518 EPoSS, 23–24.

519 See also WEBER, Information Society, 144.

520 See EPoSS, 23; for the reduction of energy use see also OECD, Towards Green ICT Strategies, June 2009, 21.

sibly market pressure created by users demanding products manufactured through processes respecting the environment.

An international agreement obliging its members to increase the use of processes respectful to the environment and scarce resources may lie somewhere in the distant future. Lessons therefore could be drawn from the Kyoto Protocol which requires mandatory emissions limitations.[521] Such an agreement would have to be ratified by States since States are then responsible to make sure that all companies and individuals situated within their territory contribute to the adherence to the agreement. The agreement itself should provide for suggestions on how to improve environmental performance, limits for energy consumption, as well as for sanctions in cases of non-compliance with the goals of the agreement. The amount of energy consumed could be verified by including the respective information in the tag attached to the object.

Through the establishment of such an agreement, scarce resources and the protection of the environment become an economic asset. Businesses that do not respect the given limits may be fined. Furthermore, businesses that do not make use of their quote could sell the left-over part to another business, thereby making a profit (as it is the case within the Kyoto Protocol[522]). The possibility of sale of quotas has to be regulated at an international level. Enterprises may be included in the preparation of a respective regulation. However, it is necessary that the public sector also has a say in the drafting of the respective agreement, as the private sector alone may favor economic interests over the environment.[523] In particular, the price for quotas has to be sufficiently elevated to make it attractive for businesses to stay under the limits prescribed by law. Therefore, limits should not be set too high – otherwise, the price for quotas on the market will decrease due to oversupply.[524]

However, while the IoT can help to reduce negative impacts on the environment, one has to make sure that the use of the IoT itself does not increase energy consumption. While this is less probable in the case of businesses that are most likely

521 Adopted December 11, 1997 and came into force on February 16, 2005; FCCP/CP/1997/L.7/Add.1; 1771 UNTS 107 (reprinted in 37 International Legal Materials 22 [1998]); for the Kyoto Protocol see e.g. Vasser Christophe P. (ed.), The Kyoto Protocol, New York 2009; Douma Wybe Th./Massai Leonardo/Montini Massimiliano, The Kyoto Protocol and Beyond, The Hague 2007; Petit Yves, Le protocole de Kyoto, Strasbourg 2002; see also OECD, Towards Green ICT Strategies, June 2009, 21.

522 See Weber Rolf H., Emissions Trading, in: Nedim Vogt/Eric Stupp/Dieter Dubs (eds), Unternehmen – Transaktion – Recht, Liber Amicorum für Rolf Watter, Zurich/St. Gallen 2008, 475–491.

523 See also Weber/Darbellay, 407.

524 See Weber/Darbellay, 405–406.

constantly connected to various networks (including in particular the Internet) with or without the existence of the IoT, the introduction of tagged objects in the lives of individuals is likely to increase energy consumption as objects have to be connected to the network at all times if they want to serve their function. Therefore, technical solutions have to be developed that allow for tags to operate on a minimal input of energy.

3. Waste Management

The tagging of every object could be very helpful when it comes to dispose of particular things. The information referred to by the tag could include information on the recycability of the object. In this context, the EU Commission intends to launch a study assessing the possibility that the presence of tags can have on the recycling of objects.[525]

However, in order to significantly increase waste management, individuals disposing of objects would have to "sign in" every bit of waste. The object's disposal can only be controlled if such action is mandatory and the individual can be warned if (s)he does not dispose of the object properly, as well as reminded where to dispose of it instead. The introduction of such control system requires major technological installation and is cannot be expected to be realized in the near future.

Nevertheless, at least for commercial and industrial waste (as opposed to municipal waste), regulations could be introduced that oblige businesses to dispose of their waste according to the information retrievable through the IoT. Such obligations would be particularly important with regard to industrial hazardous waste that causes a threat to human or environmental health.

While respective mechanisms could improve waste management, potential difficulties in the disposal of the tags themselves also need to be considered. Therefore, tags have to be produced that are environmentally neutral or made of decomposable materials.[526] However, considering the fact that tags can potentially have an extremely long life span (if the objects they are attached to are not disposed of), tags made of decomposable materials may not be appropriate and the possibility of environmentally neutral tags has to be concretized.

---

525 Communication of June 18, 2009 on the "Internet of Things – An action plan for Europe", COM (2009) 278 final.

526 ANEC/BEUC, 8.

E. Improving Health Conditions

The IoT can improve various aspects concerning the health of individuals.[527] Logistics processes as well as care-taking in hospitals can be improved, based on the traceability of everything from blood to joint hips, equipment, as well as people, in particular new-born babies.[528]

With the IoT, things can become more and more integrated within the human body. It is expected that body area networks are able to be formed communicating with treating physicians, emergency services, and humans caring elderly people. This development is not new. An existing example can already be seen in the Cardioverter-Defibrillator, which is built into the human heart, and is capable of autonomously deciding on when to administer shocks to defibrillate, and is fully networked such that a doctor can follow up on his patient.[529]

Implantable wireless identifiable devices could be used to store health records that are likely to save a patient's life in emergency situations. Being able to access the information on these situations, hospitals would know immediately how to treat an incoming patient. This possibility is especially useful for people with diabetes, cancer, coronary heart disease, stroke, chronic obstructive pulmonary disease, cognitive impairments, seizure disorders and Alzheimer's as well as people with complex medical device implants, such as pacemakers, stents, joint replacements and organ transplants and who may be unconscious and unable to communicate for themselves while in the operating theatre.[530]

Furthermore, information about patients and health status allows for hospitals to check before giving medication to a patient whether it is the right drug, at the right time, and in the right dosage based on the age, weight and height of the patient.[531] Drug compatibility can be ensured by assigning codes to drug packages, thereby building a drug knowledge base which alarms people of allergies or interferences with other drugs.[532] The IoT as a tool to combat counterfeiting also improves the health of individuals, as it can be ensured that people are not taking counterfeited – and potentially lethal – medications.[533]

Savings and improvements of life through the IoT are also possible with regard to the prediction of weather conditions and to the circumvention of other accidents.

527 For the negative impacts of the IoT on health see above IV.E.3.2.b.
528 HALLER/KARNOUSKOS/SCHROTH, 20.
529 European Commission, Strategic Research Roadmap, para. 2.5.
530 European Commission, Strategic Research Roadmap, para. 2.5.
531 AHLE, 340–342.
532 CHIAKI ISHIKAWA, YRP, at the CASAGRAS conference in London on October 6–7, 2009.
533 See above V.C.

Human life can be spared through early warnings, and people saved from accidents if they are informed of dangerous situations. This fact, in turn, also benefits insurances, which can minimize the risks. Therefore, the question is legitimate whether insurances should contribute to the costs of the IoT, as they also benefit from its advantages at a later stage. However, determining the exact amount of financial contribution to the development IoT will be challenging.

Even bigger are the savings stemming from the benefits of ambient assisted living, which allows for people to stay at home for a longer period of time. In particular with the expected ageing of society and the associated rise of health care costs, the IoT can become beneficial.[534]

F. Securing Food Supply

The IoT makes improvements in the field of food with regard to two aspects. Firstly, it can ensure fresh goods delivery and food traceability. Secondly, the global food crisis may be stemmed with the introduction of the IoT.

Traceability of food products helps the users to verify the origin of a product, thereby preserving agricultural diversity and rural lifestyles. Furthermore, information on the origin, the use of chemicals etc. may also prevent from unwanted diseases. Early warnings help assuring the users that the food they buy is of controlled origin, and that the quality control extends from the farm through shops and public authorities to the table. This automation protects people from catching diseases such as Bovine Spongiform Encephalopathy (BSE) or bird flu. Furthermore, in case of the detection of an infected product, the origin can be traced faster and its impact curbed better and faster.[535]

The US company Dole is using RFID to track its fresh produce, in particular lettuce, as it moved from the farm fields through the processing facility and, ultimately, to the store shelf. Dole introduced this measure in response to the September 2006 crisis in which some of its bagged spinach was implicated in the outbreak of Escherichia coli, a bacterium, which killed three people and sickened hundreds more.[536]

The use of RFID not only helps large companies keep tight track of inventory, but also to lower costs by limiting recalls to only the products that are at risk. For instance, in Dole's case, the company did not have to recall every single bag of

534 HALLER/KARNOUSKOS/SCHROTH, 20.

535 EPoSS, 15; SAKAMURA, 21–22.

536 See http://www.fool.com/investing/value/2007/09/20/rfid-saves-the-dole.aspx.

spinach across North America. Furthermore, by being able to take such prompt action, Dole was in the position to reduce its exposure to legal liability issues.[537]

Traceability of production can also provide market feedback to the producers in a sector where production is often planned well in advance according to predictions. This results in limited flexibility of producers. The global food crisis demonstrates that the current feedback mechanisms in the food market do not work sufficiently well, resulting in food overproduction and food shortage. These predictions could be improved through the IoT, allowing for farmers to time their produce and offerings better to market demand fluctuations. The possibility of food supply stability must not be underestimated in a time where hunger is still a major concern (particularly) in developing countries.[538]

G. Monitoring Compliance with Labor Standards

The information referred to by the tagged item could also point to labor conditions in the production of the respective object. Adherence to international labor standards (such as the prohibition of forced and child labor, the right to organize and collective bargaining, or the right to equal remuneration) is particularly an issue in developing countries. Users in developed countries are often interested in the production methods and would therefore appreciate information on labor standards provided by businesses situated in developing countries. The IoT would serve as an ideal platform for the distribution of such information.

The inclusion of information on labor standards presupposes an existing monitoring mechanism within companies. Monitors have to be independent – external monitoring carried out by certified organizations or NGOs seems most appropriate.[539]

The requirement to adhere to fundamental labor standards is also important with regard to fair competition.[540] As companies situated in developing countries get more and more involved in the global exchange of goods[541], upholding the principle of fair competition deserves a special focus and the IoT with its ability to

[537] See http://www.fool.com/investing/value/2007/09/20/rfid-saves-the-dole.aspx.

[538] EPoSS, 15.

[539] For the monitoring of the prohibition of child labor in the business sector see WEBER ROMANA, Transnational Corporations and Child Labor, forthcoming.

[540] See also WEBER ROLF H./WEBER ROMANA, Unlauteres Marktverhalten des Importeurs bei Nichteinhaltung von Arbeitsbedingungen durch ausländische Lieferanten?, GRUR International, 2008, 899–906.

[541] For the digital divide see above V.A.

provide globally accessible information on goods and their methods of production constitutes an opportunity not to be neglected.

VI. Concluding Observations

The IoT is a newly emerging framework based on the Internet, which can, amongst other functions, contribute to the global exchange of goods. While various technologies have to be kept in mind, the tagging of objects with RFID chips seems to be the favourite approach at the moment. These tags allow for the introduction of an EPC that can subsequently refer to the information about the product which is stored on the Internet and which can be accessed through the ONS or an EPC Discovery Service.

The IoT should be decentralized and interoperable in order to avoid a single entity having total control over the framework. Furthermore, a decentralized structure also decreases the danger of a single point of failure.

The IoT as a global structure is in the position to stimulate competition. On the one hand, the inclusion of companies from developing countries forces enterprises from developed countries to reconsider their practices and make a bigger effort and possibly increase their innovative endeavours to stay competitive. Furthermore, an increase of information for businesses also results in competitive advantages in terms of process optimization. On the other hand, such information about goods can also harm competition by businesses infringing intellectual property provisions, which may lead to a decrease in innovations. Accordingly, solutions – in particular legal solutions – have to be found in order to allow for the IoT to emerge as a global framework without suffering from major drawbacks.

The IoT will most likely be self-regulated. Notwithstanding the fact that self-regulation also suffers from weaknesses, it is easier to establish than binding law, and can be more easily adjusted to new developments which are particularly important in technological environments that are continuously evolving. Nevertheless, the most fundamental guidelines should be established on a legally binding basis, preferably by an international legislator (considering the global accessibility of the IoT). This international legislator could either be newly established, or be introduced as a Committee of an already existing international organization. In particular the WTO or the OECD would be appropriate to include such a body. The EU has already issued staff papers concerning the IoT, from which lessons can be drawn. Nevertheless, the discussion has to be global and solutions should not be geographically limited.

Security and privacy are of a particular importance in the IoT. Business transactions and interests of enterprises involved have to be kept confidential in order to protect businesses themselves as well as fair competition. The resulting challenges can be encountered by introducing PET, which increase security and privacy on a technological basis. However, these measures are not sufficient to pro-

R.H. Weber and R. Weber, *Internet of Things*, DOI 10.1007/978-3-642-11710-7_6,

tect users. A legal approach also has to be considered. As the right to privacy is considered a fundamental right, lessons can be drawn from the more general discussions on human rights' application. While existing regulations concerning security and privacy need to be adhered to in the future, too, the introduction of new provisions seems to be inevitable. These provisions should include rules on liability for bodies violating the right to privacy. Finally, users of the IoT also need to be informed of potential dangers and how to avoid them, as they themselves are in the position to substantially contribute to their own security and privacy.

Another aspect that must be addressed by regulatory approaches is the governance of the IoT. To this aspect, lessons can be drawn from the discourses on Internet Governance. All bodies involved in the functioning of the IoT should be subjected to certain guidelines concerning governance. In particular, bodies have to be legitimate and include all stakeholders. Furthermore, stakeholders have to be able to pronounce their views on the functioning of the IoT and be heard by the governing bodies. In addition, bodies need to be transparent and accountable. Accountability of governing bodies is even more important in the IoT than it is in the Internet, because it is essential for businesses to know that their transactions will be carried out. If business transactions fail because of faults in the system, businesses should be able to ascertain whom to hold responsible. Furthermore, the problem of critical resources has to be addressed. Infrastructure requirements are to be met, i.e. systems need to be robust, available, reliable and interoperable to allow for the IoT to serve as a global framework for the exchange of goods. In addition, access to the infrastructure has to be provided. Particularly, an equitable and non-discriminatory use of the IoT by all interested businesses should be achieved. The right to access can also be seen based on the essential facilities doctrine.

There are still a few barriers to the IoT that need to be overcome in order for the IoT to become fully operable. Multi-lingualism is an issue in the IoT as it also is in the Internet, and lessons can be drawn from there. Furthermore, legal barriers have to be addressed, in particular the regulation of radio frequency which is subject to national legislation, but which requires a certain harmonization in order to allow for RFID tags to be globally readable and not to interfere with other services such as radio or television. Concerns also exist regarding health impacts of RFID tags outputting electromagnetic energy or interfering with other devices. These concerns have to be taken seriously and be addressed, preferably by an organization knowledgeable of technology as well as of human health.

While these difficulties still have to be tackled, one needs to keep in mind the numerous benefits of the IoT. In particular, the IoT can contribute to the bridging of the digital divide by including enterprises in developing countries in the global exchange of goods. Furthermore, the introduction of search engines in the IoT allows for users to find and access the requested information in a short time span, which increases the benefits of the IoT for all users, but in particular inexperienced users. The IoT also contributes to the combat of product counterfeiting, sustainable environment, a decrease in energy consumption and waste management. An improvement of health conditions that can be achieved by using the IoT, securing food supply by ensuring fresh goods delivery and food traceability, as well as stemming of the global food crisis contributes to global welfare. Finally, the IoT allows for a monitoring of compliance with labor standards, which is particularly important in developing countries.

Keeping in mind all the courses of action that should be taken according to this research project, it is important to note that these considerations have been made at the very beginning of the IoT as a global framework. Future research and adaption of proposed models is inevitable, and will help ensure that the IoT becomes a successful operation.

Publikationen aus dem Zentrum für Informations- und Kommunikationsrecht der Universität Zürich

erschienen bei Schulthess Juristische Medien AG, Zürich

Band 1 **Neues Fernmelderecht – Erste Orientierung**
WEBER ROLF H. (Hrsg.),
mit Beiträgen von Fischer Peter R., Geiser Jean-Maurice, Gunter Pierre-Yves, Haag Marcel, Hoffet Franz, Maurer François, Ramsauer Matthias, Rieder Pierre, Stampfli Katharina und Weber Rolf H., Zürich 1998

Band 2 **Symposium Schluep – Querbezüge zwischen Kommunikations- und Wettbewerbsrecht**
WEBER ROLF H. (HRSG.),
in Zusammenarbeit mit von der Crone Hans Caspar, Forstmoser Peter, Zäch Roger und Zobl Dieter,
mit Beiträgen von von der Crone Hans Caspar/Groner Roger, Mestmäcker Ernst-Joachim, Nobel Peter, Schwarz Mathias/Klingner Norbert und Weber Rolf H., Zürich 1998

Band 3 **Informatik und Jahr 2000 – Risiken und Vorsorgemöglichkeiten aus rechtlicher Sicht**
WEBER ROLF H.
Zürich 1998

Band 4 **Daten und Datenbanken – Rechtsfragen zu Schutz und Nutzung**
WEBER ROLF H./HILTY RETO M. (Hrsg.),
mit Beiträgen von Druey Jean Nicolas, Gaster Jens-L., Hilty Reto M., Kemper Kurt, Sieber Ulrich und Weber Rolf H., Zürich 1998

Band 5 **Neustrukturierung der Rundfunkordnung**
WEBER ROLF H.
Zürich 1999

Band 6 **Rechtsschutz von Datenbanken (EU – USA – Schweiz)**
KÜBLER PHILIP
Zürich 1999

Band 7 **Informationsqualität – Ein Beitrag zur journalistischen Qualitätsdebatte aus der Sicht des Informationsrechts**
ZULAUF RENA
Zürich 2000

Band 8 **Werbung im Internet – Rechtsvergleichende, lauterkeitsrechtliche Beurteilung von Werbeformen**
JÖHRI YVONNE
Zürich 2000

Band 9 **Rechtlicher Regelungsrahmen von raumbezogenen Daten**
WEBER ROLF H.
Zürich 2000

Band 10 **Geschäftsplattform Internet – Rechtliche und praktische Aspekte**
WEBER ROLF H./HILTY RETO M./AUF DER MAUR ROLF (Hrsg.)
Zürich 2000

Band 11 **Finanzierung der Rundfunkordnung**
WEBER ROLF H.
Zürich 2000

Band 12 **Der Softwarepflegevertrag**
WIDMER MICHAEL
Zürich 2000

Band 13 **Datenschutzrecht vor neuen Herausforderungen**
Marketing – E-Commerce – Virtuelle Bank – Sachdaten
WEBER ROLF H.
Zürich 2000

Band 14 **Geschäftsplattform Internet II – Rechtliche und praktische Aspekte**
WEBER ROLF H./HILTY RETO M./AUF DER MAUR ROLF (Hrsg.)
Zürich 2001

Band 15 **Digitale Verbreitung von Rundfunkprogrammen und Meinungsvielfalt – Entwicklungen, Probleme, Lösungen**
WEBER ROLF H./DÖRR BIANKA S.
Zürich 2001

Band 16 **Die Übernahme von Allgemeinen Geschäftsbedingungen in elektronisch abgeschlossene Verträge**
SCHWAB KARIN
Zürich 2001

Band 17 **Geschäftsplattform Internet III – Kapitalmarkt – Marktauftritt – Besteuerung**
WEBER ROLF H./HILTY RETO M./AUF DER MAUR ROLF (Hrsg.)
Zürich 2002

Band 18 **Rechtliche Rahmenbedingungen für verwaltungsunabhängige Behördenkommissionen – Untersuchung am Beispiel der geplanten Fernmelde- und Medienkommission**
WEBER ROLF H./BIAGGINI GIOVANNI
Mitarbeit: Dörr Bianka S./Peduzzi Roberto
Zürich 2002

Band 19 **Elektronische Signaturen**
SCHLAURI SIMON
Zürich 2002

Band 20 **Zugang zu Kabelnetzen – Spannungsfeld zwischen Netzbetreiberfreiheit und offenem Zugang**
WEBER ROLF H.
Zürich 2003

Band 21 **Elektronische Signaturen und Haftung der Anbieter von Zertifizierungsdiensten – Eine Darstellung am Beispiel der Regelungen in der EU, Deutschland, Grossbritannien und der Schweiz**
Dörr Bianka S.
Zürich 2003

Band 22 **Geschäftsplattform Internet IV**
Weber Rolf H./Berger Mathis/Auf der Maur Rolf (Hrsg.)
Zürich 2003

Band 23 **IT-Outsourcing**
ICT: Rechtspraxis I
Weber Rolf H./Berger Mathis/Auf der Maur Rolf (Hrsg.)
Zürich 2003

Band 24 **Rechtsfragen rund um Suchmaschinen**
Weber Rolf H.
Mitarbeit: Spacek Dirk
Zürich 2003

Band 25 **Schweizerisches Filmrecht**
Weber Rolf H./Unternährer Roland/Zulauf Rena
Zürich 2003

Band 26 **Kinofilmverwertung in der Schweiz**
Unternährer Roland
Zürich 2003

Band 27 **E-Health und Datenschutz**
Berger Kurzen Brigitte
Zürich 2004

Band 28 **Unternehmensinformation und Recht – Eine Übersicht**
Stückelberger Balz
Zürich 2004

Band 29 **Schutz von TV-Formaten – Eine rechtliche und ökonomische Betrachtung**
Spacek Dirk
Zürich 2005

Band 30 **Kulturquoten im Rundfunk**
Weber Rolf H./Rossnagel Alexander/Osterwalder Simon/Scheuer Alexander/Wüst Sonia
Zürich 2006

Band 31 **Zugang zu Premium Content**
Weber Rolf H./Osterwalder Simon
Zürich 2006

Band 32 **Sorgfaltspflichten bei der Datenübertragung**
Favre Katia
Zürich 2006

Band 33 **IT-Sicherheit und Recht – Grundlagen eines integrativen Gestaltungskonzepts**
WEBER ROLF H./WILLI ANNETTE
Zürich 2006

Band 34 **Privatvervielfältigung im digitalen Umfeld**
BAUMGARTNER TOBIAS
Zürich 2006

Band 35 **Das Recht der personenbezogenen Information**
WEBER ROLF H./SOMMERHALDER MARKUS
Zürich 2007

Band 36 **Staatliche Massnahmen gegen Medienkonzentration**
KELLERMÜLLER HANSPETER
Zürich 2007

Band 37 **Der Mehrwertdienst im Fernmelderecht**
HUBER KARIN
Zürich 2007

Band 38 **Telecommunications Competition and Its Driving Force**
WU JUN
Zürich 2008

Band 39 **Media Governance und Service Public**
WEBER ROLF H.
Zürich 2007

Band 40 **The Information Society and the Digital Divide Legal Strategies to Finance Global Access**
WEBER ROLF H./MENOUD VALÉRIE A.
Zürich 2008

Band 41 **Netzzugang in der Telekommunikation**
AMGWERD MATTHIAS
Zürich 2008

Band 42 **IT-Governance als Aufgabe des Verwaltungsrates – Kriterien einer sorgfältigen Pflichterfüllung unter Berücksichtigung der strategischen Rolle der IT im Unternehmen**
WILLI ANNETTE
Zürich 2008

Band 43 **Der ASP-Vertrag**
CHRISTIAN M. IMHOF
Zürich 2008

Band 44 **Zivilrechtliche Haftung von Internet-Providern bei Rechtsverletzungen durch ihre Kunden**
FRECH PHILIPP
Zürich 2009

Band 45 **Public Key Infrastructure**
MARKWALDER DANIEL
Zürich 2009

Band 46 **Shaping Internet Governance: Regulatory Challenges**
WEBER ROLF H.
Zürich 2009

Band 47 **Rundfunkübertragungsrechte an den Olympischen Spielen im europäischen Kartellrecht**
Medienmärkte, gemeinsamer Erwerb durch die European Broadcasting Union und Exklusivvergabe
IRENE HELLWIG
Zürich 2009

Ausserdem erschienen:

Regulatory Models for the Online World
WEBER ROLF H.
Zürich 2002

Towards a Legal Framework for the Information Society
WEBER ROLF H.
in collaboration with Roduner Xenia
Zürich 2003

FSC
www.fsc.org
MIX
Papier | Fördert
gute Waldnutzung
FSC® C083411

Kolibri 360 GmbH
Ferdinand-Jühlke-Straße 7
99095 Erfurt, Deutschland
produktsicherheit@kolibri360.de